The Inner Life

ANDREW MURRAY

Whitaker House

PITTSBURGH and COLFAX STS SPRINGDALE PA 15144

THE INNER LIFE

ISBN: 0-88368-138-2
Printed in the United States of America
Copyright © 1984 by Whitaker House
Cover photo by: Fred Sieb

Whitaker House
580 Pittsburgh Street
Springdale, PA 15144

5 6 7 8 9 10 11 12 13 14 / 06 05 04 03 02 01 00 99 98 97 96

CONTENTS

PREFACE

The daily need for a time of solitude and quiet to pray and read God's Word is of utmost importance. This time spent in fellowship with God will bring a blessing, strengthen our spiritual life, and prepare us to meet the world. Then, we will be equipped for service in God's Kingdom in soul-winning and intercession. In this book I have attempted to systematically discuss the various aspects of the *inner life*. I hope that these lessons will help you in the cultivation of the hidden life and your relationship with God.

In the country of South Africa there are various diseases that affect the orange trees. One of them is popularly known by the name of the root disease. A tree may be bearing fruit, and an ordinary observer may not notice anything wrong. However, an expert can see the beginning of a slow death. This disease also affects the vineyards, and only one cure has been found. That is to take out the old roots and provide new ones. The old vine is grafted onto a new root. In time you will have the same stem and branches and fruit as before, but the roots are new and able to resist the disease. The disease comes in the part of the plant that is hidden from sight, and that is where healing must also take place.

The Church of Christ and the spiritual life of thousands of its members suffer from root disease—the neglect of secret communion with God. It is the lack of secret prayer, the neglect of the maintenance of a hidden life "rooted and grounded in love" (Ephesians 3:17), that explains the inability of the Christian life to resist the world and its failure to produce fruit abundantly. Nothing can change this except the restoration of the inner chamber in the life of the believer. As Christians learn to daily sink their roots deeper into Christ and to make secret personal fellowship with God their main priority, true godliness will flourish. "If the root be holy, so are the branches" (Romans 11:16). If the morning hour is made holy to the Lord, the day with its duties will also be holy. If the root is healthy, the branches will be, too. I pray that God may bless this book to His children who are in the pursuit of the deeper and more fruitful life, the life hid with Christ in God.

Andrew Murray

Chapter 1

THE MORNING HOUR

"My voice shalt thou hear in the morning, O Lord; in the morning will I direct my prayer unto thee, and will look up"—Psalm 5:3.

"The Lord God. . .wakeneth morning by morning, he wakeneth mine ear to hear as the learned"—Isaiah 50:4.

Morning has always been considered the time best suited for personal worship by God's servants. Most Christians regard it as a duty and a privilege to devote some portion of the beginning of the day to seek fellowship with God. Many Christians observe the morning watch, while others speak of it as the quiet hour, the still hour, or the quiet time. All these, whether they think of a whole hour or half an hour or a quarter of an hour, agree with the Psalmist when he says, "My voice shalt Thou hear in the morning, O Lord."

The Importance Of The Morning Watch

In speaking of the extreme importance of this daily time of quiet for prayer and meditation on

God's Word, a well-known Christian leader has said: "Next to receiving Christ as Savior and claiming the baptism of the Holy Spirit, we know of no act that brings greater good to ourselves or others than the determination to keep the morning watch, and spend the first half hour of the day alone with God." At first glance this statement appears too strong. The firm determination to keep the morning watch hardly appears sufficiently important to be compared to receiving Christ and the baptism of the Holy Spirit. However, it is true that it is impossible to live our daily Christian life, or maintain a walk in the leading and power of the Holy Spirit, without a daily, close fellowship with God. The morning watch is the key to the position in which the surrender to Christ and the Holy Spirit can be unceasingly and fully maintained.

The morning watch must not be regarded as an end in itself. Although it gives us a blessed time for prayer and Bible study and brings us a certain measure of refreshment and help, that is not enough. It is to serve to secure the presence of Christ for the whole day.

Personal devotion to a friend or a pursuit means that they will always hold a place in our heart, even when other people and things occupy our attention. Personal devotion to Jesus means that we allow nothing to separate us from Him for a moment. To abide in Him and His love, to be kept by Him and His grace, to be doing His will and pleasing Him—this cannot possibly be an irregular practice if we are truly devoted to Him.

"I need Thee every hour," "Moment by moment I am kept in His love." These hymns are the language of life and truth. "In Thy name shall they rejoice all the day" (Psalm 89:16). "I the Lord do keep it; I will water it every moment" (Isaiah 27:3). These are words of divine power. The believer cannot stand for one moment without Christ. Personal devotion to Him refuses to be content with anything less than to abide always in His love and His will. This is the true scriptural Christian life. The importance and blessedness and true aim of the morning watch can only be realized as our personal devotion becomes its chief purpose.

Securing His Presence

The clearer the objective of our pursuit, the better we will be able to adapt to attain it. Consider the morning watch now as the means to this great end: I want to secure the presence of Christ all the day, to do nothing that can interfere with it. I feel that my success during the day will depend upon my time spent alone with Him in the morning. Meditation and prayer and the Word are secondary to this purpose: renewing the link for the day between Christ and me in the morning hour.

Concern for the day ahead, with all its possible cares, pleasures, and temptations, may seem to disturb the rest I have enjoyed in my quiet devotion. This is possible, but it will be no loss. True Christianity aims at having the character of Christ so formed in us, that in our most ordinary activities

9

His temperament and attitudes reveal themselves. The Spirit and the will of Christ should so possess us that in our relationships with people, in our leisure time, and in our daily business it will be second nature for us to act like Him. All this is possible because Christ Himself, as the Living One, lives in us.

Do not be disturbed if at first this goal appears too difficult and occupies too much of your time in the hour of private prayer. The time you give to bring your daily concerns to the Lord will be richly rewarded. You will return to prayer and Scripture reading with new purpose and new faith. As the morning watch begins to have its effects on the day, the day will respond to its first half hour, and fellowship with Christ will have new meaning and power.

Wholehearted Determination

As we seek to have this unbroken fellowship with God in Christ throughout the day, we will realize that only a definite meeting time with Christ will secure His presence for the day. The one essential thing to having this daily quiet time is wholehearted *determination,* whatever effort or self-denial it may cost, to win the prize. In academic study or in athletics, every student needs *determined* purpose to succeed. Christianity requires, and indeed deserves, not less but more intense devotion. If anything, surely the love of Christ needs the whole heart.

It is this fixed decision to secure Christ's presence that will overcome every temptation to be unfaithful or superficial in the keeping of our pledges. This *determination* will make the morning watch itself a mighty force in strengthening our character and giving us boldness to resist self-indulgence. It will enable us to enter the inner chamber and shut the door for our communion with Christ. From the morning watch on, this firm resolution will become the keynote of our daily life.

In the world it is often said: Great things are possible to any man who knows what he wills and wills it with all his heart. The believer who has made personal devotion to Christ his watchword will find in the morning hour the place where day by day the insight into his holy calling is renewed. During this quiet time, his will is fortified to walk worthy of his calling. His faith is rewarded by the presence of Christ who is waiting to meet him and take charge of him for the day. We are more than conquerors through Him who loves us. A living Christ waits to meet us.

Chapter 2

FELLOWSHIP WITH THE FATHER

"When thou prayest, enter into thy closet, shut thy door, pray to thy Father which is in secret"—Matthew 6:6.

Man was created for fellowship with God. God made him in His own image and likeness, so he would be capable of understanding and enjoying God, entering into His will, and delighting in His glory. Because God is the everywhere-present and all-pervading One, man could have lived in the enjoyment of this unbroken fellowship.

Sin *robbed us of this fellowship.* Nothing but this fellowship can satisfy the heart of either man or God. It was this fellowship that Christ came to restore; to bring back to God His lost creature, and to bring man back to all he was created for. Fellowship with God is the consummation of all blessedness on earth as it is in heaven. This blessing comes when we experience the promise: "I will never leave thee nor forsake thee" (Hebrews 13:5), and when we can say: The Father is always with me.

This fellowship with God is meant to be ours all day long, whatever our condition or the circumstances surrounding us. The ability to maintain close and glad fellowship with God all day long will depend entirely upon the intensity with which we seek Him in the hour of secret prayer. The one essential thing in the morning watch or the quiet hour is—fellowship with God.

Meet The Father

Our Lord teaches us the inner secret of prayer: "Shut thy door and pray to thy Father which is in secret." When you are in secret you have the Father's presence and attention. You know that He sees and hears you. Of more importance than all your requests is this one thing—the childlike, living assurance that your Father sees you and that you have now met Him face to face. With His eye on you and yours on Him, you are now enjoying actual fellowship with Him.

Christian, there is a terrible danger to which you stand exposed in your inner chamber of prayer. You are in danger of substituting prayer and Bible study for living fellowship with God. Fellowship is the living interchange of giving Him your love, your heart, and your life and receiving from God His love, His life, and His Spirit. Your needs and their expression, your desire to pray humbly, earnestly, and believingly, may so occupy your mind that the light of His countenance and the joy of His love cannot enter you. Your Bible study may so interest you that the very Word of

God may become a substitute for God Himself. The greatest hindrance to fellowship is anything that keeps the soul occupied instead of leading it to God Himself. We go out into the day's work without the power of an abiding fellowship, because the blessing was not secured in our morning devotions.

Give Him Your Day

What a difference it would make in the life of many Christians if everything in the closet were subordinate to this one decision: I want to walk with God throughout the day and my morning hour is the time when my Father enters into a definite relationship with me and I with Him. What strength would be imparted to us if we could say: God has taken charge of me; He is going with me Himself; I am going to do His will all day in His strength; I am ready for all that may come. Yes, what a change would come into our life if secret prayer were not only an asking for knowledge or strength, but the giving of our life for one day into the safe keeping of a faithful God.

"Pray to the Father which is in secret, and thy Father which seeth in secret shall reward thee openly" (Matthew 6:6). When secret fellowship with the Father is maintained, in spirit and in truth, our public life before people will carry the reward. The Father who sees in secret takes charge and rewards openly. Separation from others, in solitude with God—this is the sure, the only way

14

to live in harmony with people in the power of God's blessing.

Chapter 3

UNBROKEN FELLOWSHIP

"When thou fastest, anoint thine head, and wash thy face; that thou appear not unto men to fast, but unto thy Father which is in secret, and thy Father which seeth in secret, shall reward thee openly"—Matthew 6:17.

"When they saw the boldness of Peter and John. . .they took knowledge of them, that they had been with Jesus"—Acts 4:13.

"And it came to pass, when Moses came down from mount Sinai . . .that (he) wist not that the skin of his face shone while he talked with him. And when Aaron and all the children of Israel saw Moses, behold, the skin of his face shone; and they were afraid to come nigh him. . . .And till Moses had done speaking with them, he put a veil on his face"—Exodus 34:29-30,33.

The transition from fellowship with God in the morning hour to interaction with our fellowmen is often difficult. If we have met God, we long to maintain the sense of His presence and our surrender to Him. Yet, when we go out to the breakfast table the atmosphere is suddenly different. As the presence of our family and material things take over, we begin to lose what we gained in our quiet time.

Maintaining The Glow

Many young Christians have wondered how to keep their heart filled with the truth when they do not have the liberty or the opportunity to speak to others. Even in religious circles it is not always easy to communicate that which would give us the greatest profit and pleasure. Let us strive to learn how our conversations with people may be, instead of a hindrance, a help to the maintenance of a life of continual fellowship with God.

The story of Moses with the veil on his face teaches us an important lesson. Close and continued fellowship with God will in due time leave its mark and manifest itself to those around us. Just as Moses did not know that his face shone, we ourselves will be unaware of the light of God shining from us. Instead, it will deepen the sense of our being an earthen vessel (see 2 Corinthians 4:6,7). The sense of God's presence in a person may often cause others to feel ill at ease in his company. However, the true believer will know what it is to veil his face and prove by humility and love that he is indeed a man like those around him. And yet, there will be the proof that he is a man of God, who lives in and has dealings with an unseen world.

This same lesson is taught by our Lord when He

spoke about fasting. Jesus said we should not draw attention to ourselves when we are fasting, "That thou appear not unto Me to fast." Expect God, who has seen you in secret, to reward you openly and to make others know that His grace and light are upon you.

The story of Peter and John confirms the same truth: they had been with Jesus not only while He was on earth, but as He entered into the heavenlies and poured out His Spirit. They simply acted out what the Spirit of Christ taught them. Even their enemies could see by their boldness that they had been with Jesus.

Unbroken Fellowship

The blessing of communion with God can easily be lost by entering too deeply into communion with people. The spirit of the inner chamber must be carried over into a holy watchfulness throughout the day. We do not know at what hour the enemy will come. This continuance of the morning watch can be maintained by quiet self-restraint, by not giving the reins of our lives over to our natural impulses.

This spirit of watchfulness can be encouraged by the other members of the family. Around the breakfast table each person in turn may quote a verse pertaining to a certain subject. This practice will provide an easy opportunity for spiritual and godly conversation. When the abiding sense of God's presence has become the aim of the morning hour, then with deep humility and in loving

18

conversation with those around us, we will pass on into the day's duties with the continuity of unbroken fellowship. It is a great thing to enter the inner chamber, shut the door, and meet the Father in secret. It is a greater thing to open the door again and go out in an enjoyment of God's presence which nothing can disturb.

To some, such a life does not seem necessary. They feel one can be a good Christian without this continual fellowship with the Father. If we are to influence the Church and the world around us, we must be full of God and His presence. Everything else must be secondary to this one question: How can we have the power of Christ resting on us all day long?

Chapter 4

PRAYER AND THE WORD OF GOD

In regard to the connection between prayer and the Word in our private devotion, this expression has often been quoted: I pray, I speak to God; I read the Bible, God speaks to me. There is a verse in the history of Moses in which this thought is beautifully brought out. We read in Numbers 7:89: "When Moses was gone into the tabernacle of the congregation to speak with Him, then he heard the voice of One speaking unto him from off the mercy seat. . .and (God) spoke unto him." When Moses went in to pray for himself or his people and to wait for instructions, he found One waiting for him. What a lesson for our morning watch.

A Prayerful Spirit

A prayerful spirit is the spirit to which God will speak. A prayerful spirit will be a listening spirit waiting to hear what God says. In true communion with God, His presence and the part He takes must be as real as my own. We need to ask how our

Scripture reading and praying can become true fellowship with God.

Get into the right place. Moses went into the tabernacle to speak with God. He separated himself from the people and went where he could be alone with God. He went to the place where God was to be found. Jesus has told us where that place is. He calls us to enter into our closet, shut the door, and pray to the Father who is in secret. Any place where we are really alone with God can be for us the secret of His presence. To speak with God requires separation from all else. It needs a heart intently set upon and in full expectation of meeting God personally and having direct dealings with Him. Those who go there to speak to God will hear the voice of One speaking to them.

Get into the right position. Moses heard the voice of One speaking from the mercy seat. Bow before the mercy seat where the awareness of your unworthiness will not hinder you, but will be a real help in trusting God. At the mercy seat you can have the assurance that your upward look will be met by His eye, that your prayer can be heard, that His loving answer will be given. Bow before the mercy seat and be sure that the God of mercy will see and bless you.

Get into the right frame of mind. Have a listening attitude. Many people are so occupied with how much or how little they have to say in their prayers that the voice of One speaking is never heard, because it is not expected or waited for. "Thus saith the Lord, The heaven is My throne, and the earth is My footstool. . .but to this man will I look, even to him that is poor and of a contrite spirit, and trembleth at My word" (Isaiah 66:1,2). Let us enter the closet, and prepare ourselves to pray, with a heart that humbly waits to hear God speak. In the Word we read that we will indeed hear the voice of One speaking to us. The greatest blessing in prayer will be our ceasing to pray and to let God speak.

Prayer And The Word

Prayer and the Word are inseparably linked together: power in the use of either depends upon the presence of the other. The Word gives me *matter* for prayer, telling me what God will do for me. It shows me the *path* of prayer, telling me how God would have me come. It gives me the *power* for prayer, the assurance that I will be heard. And it brings me the *answer* to prayer, as it teaches what God will do for me. Prayer prepares the heart for receiving the Word from God Himself, for the teaching of the Spirit to give the spiritual understanding of it, for the faith that is made partaker of its mighty working.

It is clear why this is so. Prayer and the Word have one common center—God. Prayer seeks God; the Word reveals God. In prayer, man asks God; in the Word, God answers man. In prayer, man rises to heaven to dwell with God; in the Word, God comes to dwell with man. In prayer, man gives himself to God; in the Word, God gives Himself to man.

In prayer and the Word, God must be all. Make God the center of your heart, the one object of your desire. Prayer and the Word will be a blessed fellowship with God, the interchange of thought and love and life: a dwelling in God and God in us. Seek God and live!

Chapter 5

LEARNING HOW TO PRAY

Moses was the first man appointed to be a teacher and leader of men. In his life we find wonderful illustrations of the place and power of intercession in the servant of God.

The Prayers Of Moses

From the time God first called him in Egypt, Moses prayed. He asked God what he was to say to the people. (See Exodus 3:11-13). Moses told Him all of his weaknesses and pleaded with God to be relieved of his mission (4:1-13). When the people accused him of increasing their burdens, he went and told God (5:22). He made all his fears known to God (6:12).

Out of this time of training, his power in prayer was born. Time after time, Pharaoh asked him to entreat the Lord for him, and deliverance came at Moses' request (see Exodus chapters 8-10). Study these passages until you understand the importance of prayer in Moses' work and God's redemption.

At the Red Sea, Moses cried to God along with the people, and the answer came (14:15). In the wilderness when the people thirsted, and when Amalek attacked them, it was also prayer that brought deliverance (17:4,11).

At Sinai, when Israel made the golden calf, it was prayer that averted the threatened destruction (32:11,14). It was more prayer that secured God's presence to go with them (33:13,14). Once again it was prayer that brought the revelation of God's glory (33:18,19). When that had been given it was fresh prayer that received the renewal of the covenant (34:9,10).

In Deuteronomy we have a wonderful summary of all Moses' prayers. We see with what intensity he prayed, and we see how in one case it was for forty days and forty nights that he fell on his face before the Lord (see Deuteronomy 9:18-26).

In Numbers we read of Moses' prayer quenching the fire of the Lord and obtaining the supply of meat (see Numbers 11:2,11-13,31,32). Moses prayed for Miriam (12:13). Prayer again saved the nation when they refused to go up to Canaan (14:17-20). Prayer brought down judgment on Korah. When God was going to consume the whole congregation, prayer made atonement (16:15,46). Prayer brought water out of the rock (20:1-11), and in answer to prayer the brazen serpent was given (21:7,8). In answer to prayer God's will was made known, and Joshua was selected Moses' successor (see chapter 27).

Study all these passages until your whole heart

is filled with the part prayer must play in the life of a person who wants to be God's servant to his fellowmen.

A Man Of Prayer

As we study Moses' life, he will become a living model for our prayer life. We will learn what we need to become an intercessor. Here are the lessons we can learn from Moses' life.

Moses was a man given up to God; zealous, yes, he was even jealous for God's honor and will. He was also a man absolutely given to his people, ready to sacrifice himself, that they might be saved. Moses was a man conscious of a divine calling to act as a mediator, to be the link, the channel of communication and of blessing, between a God in heaven and men on earth. His life was so entirely possessed by this mediatorial consciousness that nothing was more simple and natural than to expect that God would hear him.

In answer to the prayers of one man, God saves and blesses those He has entrusted to him and does what He would not do without prayer. The whole government of God has taken prayer into its plan as one of its constituent parts. Heaven is filled with the life and power and blessing earth needs, and the prayer of earth is the power to bring that blessing down.

Prayer is an index of the spiritual life, and its power depends on my relationship to God and the awareness of my being His representative. He entrusts His work to me. The more simple and complete my devotion to His interests, the more natural and certain becomes the assurance that He hears me.

Think of the place God had in Moses' life, as the God who had sent him and the God to whom he was completely devoted. He was the God who promised to be with him and who would always help him when he prayed.

Learning To Pray

How can we learn to pray like Moses? We cannot secure this gift by an act of the will. Our first lesson must be the sense of our own weakness. Then grace can work in us, slowly and surely, if we give ourselves its training. The training will be gradual, but there is one thing that can be done at once. We can decide to give ourselves to this life and assume the right position. Do this now, make the decision to live entirely to be a channel for God's blessing to flow through you to the world. Take the step. Accept the divine appointment and concentrate on some particular object of intercession.

Take time, say a week, and get a firm hold on the elementary truths Moses' example teaches. Just as a music teacher insists upon practicing the scales—only practice makes perfect—determine to learn and to apply these important first lessons.

God is looking for people through whom He can bless the world. Say definitely: Here am I; I will give my life to this calling. Cultivate your faith in the simple truth: God hears prayer; God will do what I ask.

Give yourself to others as completely as you give yourself to God. Open your eyes to sense the needs of a perishing world. Take up your position in Christ and in the power which His name and life and Spirit give you. And go on practicing definite prayer and intercession.

Chapter 6

BECOMING A MAN OR WOMAN OF GOD

"Moses, the man of God, blessed the children of Israel" —Deuteronomy 33:1.

The man of God! How much this name means! He is a man who comes from God, chosen and sent by Him. He walks with God, lives in His fellowship, and carries the mark of His presence. He is a man who lives for God and His will. His whole being is ruled by the glory of God, and he involuntarily and unceasingly causes men to think of God. In his heart the life of God has taken its rightful place as the all in all. His one desire is that God should have that place of prominence in men's hearts throughout the world.

Wanted: Men Of God

Such men of God are what the world needs. God seeks these men that He may fill them with Himself and send them into the world to help others to know Him. Moses was such a man of God that men naturally spoke of him this way—Moses, the man of God! Every servant of God should strive to be a living witness of what God is to him, and what He claims to be in all.

In a previous chapter we said that man was to have fellowship with God. This fellowship is to be the privilege of our daily life and should be our highest priority during our morning time of devotions. We mainly referred to our personal need and how the power of a happy, godly life can influence others. The thought of a man like Moses leads us beyond our own personal needs. He was so closely linked to God that men by instinct gave this as his chief characteristic—the man of God! This thought brings us out into public life and suggests the idea of the impression we make upon men. We can be so full of God's holy presence that, when men see us or think of us, this name will come to mind—*the man of God.*

These are the kind of men and women the world and God equally need. Why is this? Because the world, by sin, has fallen away from God. Because in Christ the world has been redeemed for God. God has no way of showing men what they ought to be except through men of God, in whom His life, His spirit, and His power are working. Man was created for God, that God might live, work, and show forth His glory in him and through him. God was to be his all in all.

The indwelling of God was to be as natural and delightful as it is strange and incomprehensible. When the redemption of Christ was completed in the descent of the Holy Spirit into the hearts of men, this indwelling was restored, and God regained possession of His home. A person can give himself completely to the presence of the Holy Spirit, not only as a power working in him, but as God dwelling in him. Then, he can become, in the deepest meaning of the word, *a man of God!* (See John 14:16,20,23 and 1 John 4:13,16.)

A Complete Man

Paul tells us that it is through the power of the Holy Scripture that the man of God is complete. This suggests that with some the life is imperfect and needs to be made perfect. "All scripture is given by inspiration of God, and is profitable for doctrine, for reproof, for correction, for instruction in righteousness, that the man of God may be perfect, thoroughly furnished unto all good works" (2 Timothy 3:16,19).

This brings us again to the morning watch as the chief time for personal Bible study. We must yield our heart and life to the Word, for its teaching, its reproof, its correction, its instruction to search and form our whole life. In this way we will come under the direct operation of God, into full communion with Him, that the man of God will be complete—furnished to every good work.

Oh, to be truly a man of God! A man who knows and proves these three things: God is all; God claims all; God works all. A man of God has seen the place God has in His universe and in men—He is the all in all! A man of God has understood that God asks and must have all. He lives only to give God His due and glory! A man of God has discov-

31

ered the great secret that God works all and seeks, like the Son of God, to live in the unceasing, blessed dependence of the Father.

Be A Man Of God

Brother and sister, seek to be a man or woman of God! Let God in the morning watch be all to you. Let God during the day be all to you. And let your life be devoted to one thing—to bring men to God, and God to men. Let it be our desire that, in His Church and in the world, God may have the place due to Him.

"If I be a man of God, then let fire come down from heaven" (2 Kings 1:10). Thus answered Elijah when the captain called him to come down. The true God is the God who answers by fire. And the true man of God is he who knows how to call down the fire because he has power with the God of heaven. Whether the fire be that of judgment or the Holy Spirit, the work of the man of God is to bring fire down to earth. What the world needs is the man of God who knows God's power and his power with God.

It is in the secret prayer habit of daily life that we learn to know our God, His fire, and our power with Him. May we know what it is to be a man of God and what it implies.

In Elijah, as in Moses, we see that being a man of God means a separation from every other interest, an entire identification with the honor of God. He is no longer a man of the world, but *a man of God*.

There is a secret feeling that all this brings more strain and sacrifice, difficulty and danger, than we are ready for. This is only true as long as we have not seen how absolute God's claim is, how blessed it is to yield to it, and how certain that God Himself will work it in us.

Turn back now and look at Moses, the man of prayer and of the Word. See how Moses grew out of these to be the man of God. See the same in the life of Elijah—the harmony between our hearing God's Word and His hearing ours. See the way in which it becomes divinely possible to be and live as *a man of God*. Then study how you can apply these to your own life.

Chapter 7

THE POWER OF GOD'S WORD

"The word of God which effectually worketh also in you that believe" —1 Thessalonians 2:13.

The value of the words of a man depends upon what I know about him. If a man promises to give me half of all he has, it greatly matters whether he is a poor man or a millionaire. One of the first requirements for fruitful Bible study is the knowledge of God as the Omnipotent One and of the power of His Word.

Creative Power

The power of God's Word is infinite. "By the word of the Lord were the heavens made. For He spake, and it was done; He commanded and it stood fast" (Psalm 33:6,9). God's power works in His Word. *God's Word has creative power and calls into existence the very thing of which it speaks.*

The Word of the living God is a living Word, and gives life. It can call into existence and make alive again that which is dead. Its quickening power can raise dead bodies, can give eternal life to dead souls. All spiritual life comes through it, for we are born of incorruptible seed by the Word of God that lives and abides forever.

This is one of the deepest secrets of the blessing of God's Word—the faith in its creative and quickening energy. The Word will work in me the very character which it commands or promises. "The word of God effectually worketh in you that believe." Nothing can resist its power when received into the heart through the Holy Spirit because it works effectually in those who believe. "The voice of the Lord is in power." Everything depends upon learning the art of receiving that Word into the heart. And in learning this art the first step is—faith in its living, its omnipotent, its creative power. By His Word "(God) calleth those things which be not as though they were" (Romans 4:17).

Hidden Power

As true as this is of all God's mighty deeds from creation to the resurrection of the dead, it is also true of every word spoken to us in His holy book. Two things keep us from believing this as we should. The one is the terrible experience of the Word being made ineffective by human wisdom, unbelief, or worldliness. The other is the neglect of the scriptural teaching that the Word is a seed. Seeds are small and may be long dormant; seeds have to be hidden; and when they sprout, they are of slow growth.

Because the action of God's Word is hidden and unobserved, we do not believe in its power. Let us make this one of our first lessons. The Word I study is the power of God unto salvation: *it will work in me all I need, all the Father asks.*

Power To Change Us

What a prospect this kind of faith will open up for our spiritual life! We will see that all the treasures and blessings of God's grace are within our reach. The Word has power to enlighten our darkness: in our hearts it will bring the light of God, the sense of His love, and the knowledge of His will. The Word can fill us with courage to conquer every enemy and to do whatever God asks us to do. The Word will cleanse, sanctify, and work in us faith and obedience. It will become in us the seed of every trait in the likeness of our Lord. Through the Word, the Spirit will lead us into all truth. It will make all that is in the Word true in us and so prepare our heart to be the habitation of the Father and the Son.

What a change would come over our relationship to God's Word and to the morning watch if we really believed this simple truth. Let us begin our training for that ministry of the Word by proving its power in our own experience. Let us begin to seek to learn the great faith lesson, the mighty power of God's Word.

The Word of God is true because God Himself will make it true in us. We have much to learn regarding what hinders that power, much to overcome to be freed from these hindrances, and much to surrender to receive that power. But all will be right if we study our Bibles with the determination to believe that *God's Word has omnipotent power in our heart* to accomplish every blessing of which it speaks.

Chapter 8

THE WORD IS A SEED

I think it may be confidently said that in all nature the best illustration for the Word of God is that of the seed. The points of resemblance between the two are quite evident. There is the apparent insignificance of the seed—a little thing as compared with the tree that springs from it. There is the life, enclosed and dormant within a husk. There is the need for suitable soil without which growth is impossible. There is the slow growth with its length of time calling for the long patience of the farmer. And there is the fruit in which the seed reproduces and multiplies itself. In all these respects, the seed teaches us precious lessons as to our use of God's Word.

Lessons From The Seed

The lesson of faith. Faith does not look at appearances. As far as we can judge, it looks most improbable that the Word of God can give life to the soul, can transform our whole character, and can fill us with strength. And yet it does. When we have learned to believe that the Word can do what it says, then we have found one of the chief secrets of Bible study. We will then receive each word as the pledge and the power of God's working on our behalf.

The lesson of labor. The seed needs to be gathered, kept, and put into the prepared soil. In the same way the mind has to gather from Scripture, understand, and pass on to the heart the words which will meet our need. *We* cannot give life or growth to the words. Nor do we need to: it is there. But we can hide the Word in our heart and keep it there, waiting for the sunshine that comes from above.

The lesson of patience. The effect of the Word on the heart is in most cases not immediate. It needs time to send out roots and grow up: Christ's words must abide in us. We must day by day increase our reserve of Bible knowledge—this is like gathering the grain in a barn. We must also watch over those words of command or promise that have special meaning for us and allow them to spread both root and branches in our heart. We need to know what kind of seed we have sowed and to cultivate a watchful but patient expectancy. In due time we shall reap if we faint not.

The lesson of fruitfulness. However insignificant that little seed from the Word of God appears, no matter how trying the slowness of its growth may be to our patience—be sure the fruit will come. The very truth and life and power of God's Word will grow and ripen within you. A seed bears a fruit which contains the same seed for new reproduction. In the same way the Word will not only bring you the fruit it promised, but that fruit will become a seed which you carry to others to give life and blessing.

The Seed In Your Heart

Not only the Word, but "the kingdom of heaven is like a seed." The Kingdom's attributes come as a hidden seed in the heart of the regenerate person. Christ is a seed. The Holy Spirit is a seed. The exceeding greatness of the power that works in us is a seed. The hidden life is there in the heart, but it is not always felt in its power. The divine glory is there, to be counted and acted on even when not felt, to be waited for in its springing forth and its growth.

As this central truth is firmly grasped and held as the law of all heavenly life on earth, the study of God's Word becomes an act of faith, surrender, and dependence upon the living God. I believe humbly, almost tremblingly, in the divine seed that there is in the Word and the power of God's Spirit to make it true in my life and experience. I yield my heart hungrily and entirely to receive this divine seed. I wait on God in absolute dependence and confidence to give the increase in a power above anything we can ask or think.

Chapter 9

KNOWING AND DOING GOD'S WORD

"But (Jesus) said, Yea rather, blessed are they that hear the word of God, and keep it"—Luke 11:28.

"If any man will do his will, he shall know"—John 7:17.

Some time ago I received a letter from an earnest Christian asking me for some hints to help him in Bible study. He wanted some guidelines as to how to begin and how to go on, so he could better understand and know the Bible. The very first thing I said to him, the thing that comes before all else, is this: In your Bible study everything will depend upon the spirit in which you approach it.

The Objective Of Bible Study

In worldly things a man is ruled and urged on by the goals he sets for himself. It is no different with the Bible. If your aim is simply to know the Bible well, you will be disappointed. If you think that thorough knowledge of the Bible will necessarily be a blessing, you are mistaken. To some it is a curse. To others it is powerless; it does not make them either holy or happy. To some it is a burden; it depresses them instead of quickening them or lifting them up.

What should be the real objective of the Bible student? Because God's Word is food, bread from heaven, the first reason for Bible study is: *a great hunger for righteousness*—a great desire to do all God's will. The Bible is a light, and the first condition to its enjoyment is *a sincere longing to walk in God's ways.*

This is what the Bible teaches us: "Blessed are they that hear the word of God *and keep it."* There is no blessedness in hearing or knowing God's Word apart from keeping it. The Word is nothing if it is not kept, obeyed, done. "If any man will *do His will,* he shall *know."* According to this saying of our Lord, all true knowledge of God's Word depends upon there first being the will to do it. God will unlock the real meaning and blessing of His Word only to those whose will is definitely set upon doing it. I must read my Bible with one purpose—"Whatsoever He saith unto you, do it" (John 2:5).

The Importance Of Words

Words stand between the will and the deed. Suppose a man wills to do something for you. Before he does it, he expresses his thought or purpose in words. Then he fulfills the words by doing what he has promised. This is also the way God works. His words have their value from what He does. In creation His Word was with the power: He spoke and it was done.

God always does what He says. David prays, "Do as Thou hast said" (2 Samuel 7:25). Solomon also says at the consecration of the temple: "Who hath with His hands fulfilled that which He spake with His mouth;" "The Lord hath performed His word that He hath spoken;" "Thou hast kept. . .that which Thou hast promised him, and spakest with Thy mouth, and hast fulfilled it with Thine hand;" "Keep. . .that which Thou hast promised him" (2 Chronicles 6:4,10,15,16).

In the writings of the prophets, God says, "I the Lord have spoken it, and I will do it" (Ezekiel 36:36). And the prophets say, "What Thou hast spoken, is done" (Jeremiah 32:24). The truth and the worth of what God promises consist in this, that *He does it*. His word of promise is meant to be done.

Doing God's Word

This is no less true of His words of command, of things which He wants us to do. If we do not do them, if we seek to know them, if we admire their beauty and praise their wisdom, but do not do them, we delude ourselves. They are meant *to be done*. It is only as we do them that their real meaning and blessing can be revealed to us. It is only as we do them that we really can grow in the divine life. "Walk worthy of the Lord unto all pleasing, being fruitful in every good work, and increasing

43

in the knowledge of God" (Colossians 1:10). We must approach God's words with the same objective God had in mind—that they should be done.

This principle is true in any pursuit of knowledge or in any kind of business. The pupil or apprentice is expected to put the lessons he receives into practice. Only then is he prepared for further teaching. In the Christian life, Bible study should be more than mere theory—more than a pleasing exercise of mind and imagination. Bible study has little value for a life of true holiness or Christlikeness until the student makes God's purpose his very own and listens when He says: "Do all that I speak."

This was the distinguishing mark of the Old Testament men of faith. "So Abram departed, as the Lord had spoken unto him" (Genesis 12:4). "As the Lord had commanded Moses, so did he" (Exodus 40:16), is the description of the man who as a servant was faithful in all his house. And of David we read: "I have found. . .a man after Mine own heart, which shall do all My will" (Acts 13:22). In Psalm 119, we hear him speaking with God about His Word and praying for divine light and teaching, always accompanied by the vow of obedience or some other expression of love and delight. It is the doing of God's will, as it was with God's own Son, that is the one secret of entrance into the favor and the mind of God.

Young Christian, when you ask God to lead you into the treasures of His Word, do it as one who presents himself a living sacrifice, *ready to do*

44

whatever God says. Seek for this with deep humility. To enjoy your food you must first be hungry. The first requirement for Bible study is a simple longing to find out what God wants you to do and the determination to do it. "If any man will do His will, he shall know"—the Word of God will be opened to him.

Chapter 10

BECOMING A DOER OF THE WORD

"Be ye doers of the word, and not hearers only, deceiving your own selves. . .he being not a forgetful hearer, but a doer of the work, this man shall be blessed in his deed"—James 1:22,25.

It is a terrible delusion to delight in hearing the Word and yet not do it. Multitudes of Christians listen to the Word of God regularly and yet do not do it. If their own children were to hear but not do what they said, they would be greatly disturbed. However, the delusion is so complete that some never know they are not living good Christian lives. What is it that deludes us in this way?

Hearing But Not Doing

One cause for this delusion is that people often mistake hearing the Word for religion or worship. The mind delights in having truth explained and their imagination is pleased with clever illustrations. To an active mind knowledge gives pleasure. A man may study some branch of science—

46

say electricity—for the enjoyment the knowledge gives him without the least intention of applying it practically. Some people go to church, enjoy the preaching, and yet do not do what God asks. The unconverted and the converted man alike are content to continue listening and saying, yet still doing the things they should not do.

Another cause for this delusion is the false teaching that we are unable to do good. The grace of Christ to enable us to obey, to keep us from sinning, and to make us holy is so little believed that people think sinning is a part of the Christian life. They think God could not possibly expect perfect obedience from them because He knows they will fail. This error erodes away any determined purpose to do all God has said. It closes the heart to any earnest desire to believe and experience all God's grace can do in us. It keeps men self-contented in the midst of sin.

Duty But Not Delight

Another reason for this delusion centers around our private Bible reading. The hearing or reading of the Bible is often regarded as a duty. We spend our five or ten minutes in the morning reading thoughtfully and attentively trying to understand what we have read. It is a duty faithfully performed which eases the conscience and gives us a sense of satisfaction. We do not realize how this attitude of duty can cause us to become hardened toward God's Word. To avoid this delusion we must approach our daily Bible reading with the desire to do and be all that God would have us to be. "Be ye doers of the word, and not hearers only, deluding your own selves."

This delusion must be fought and conquered during our morning quiet time. This new approach may disturb our regular Bible reading and cause us to get behind in our scheduled selections. However, the important thing is that we decide to do what we read. Our Lord Jesus said: "If any man will do His will, he shall know of the doctrine whether it be of God" (John 7:17). If we delight in God's law and set our will on doing it, then we can receive divine illumination on the teachings of Christ. Without this will to do, our knowledge has little value. It is simply head knowledge.

In all of life, whether science, art, or business, the only way of truly knowing is doing. What a man cannot do, he does not thoroughly know. The only way to know God is to do His will. By doing His will, I prove whether it is a God of my own sentiment and imagination that I confess or the true and living God who rules and works over all. It is only by doing His will that I prove I love His will and accept it as my own. The only way to be united to God is to do His will.

The self-delusion of hearing and not doing is conquered in the quiet of my inner chamber. During my private Bible reading, I must decide that *I am going to do whatever God says.*

Doing God's Word

It may help us if we take a portion of God's Word and see how we can accomplish this new resolution.

Let us take the Sermon on the Mount. The first beatitude says: "Blessed are the poor in spirit" (Matthew 5:3). I ask myself, what does this mean? Am I obeying this injunction? Am I earnestly seeking day by day to maintain this attitude? As I realize how proud and self-confident my nature is, am I willing to wait, pray, and believe that He can work it in me? Am I going to do this—be poor in spirit? Or shall I be a hearer and not a doer?

In this manner, I can go through the beatitudes and the whole sermon with its teachings on meekness and mercy, on love and righteousness. As I read about trusting Him and doing His will, I must verse by verse ask myself: Do I know what this means? Am I living it? Am I doing what He says? By asking these questions I will realize the need for a change in my attitudes and my behavior. I must ask myself if the vow, *whatever He says, I am going to do,* has taken the place in my Bible reading and my life which He demands that it should have.

Before I know it such questions will give me an entirely new insight into my need for Christ who will breathe in me His own life and work in me all He speaks. I will have courage to say by faith: I can do all things through Him who strengthens me. Whatever He says in His Word, I will do.

Chapter 11

KEEPING CHRIST'S COMMANDMENTS

"If ye know these things, happy are ye if ye do them"—John 13:17.

The joy and the blessing of God's Word is only to be known by doing it. This subject is of such supreme importance in the Christian life, and therefore in our Bible study, that I must ask you to return to it once more. Let us this time just take the one expression, *keeping the Word,* or keeping the commandments.

Keep His Commandments

In Jesus' farewell address to His disciples, He emphasized the importance of keeping His commandments.

"If ye love Me, keep My commandments, and He (the Father) shall give you another Comforter" (John 14:15,16).

"He that hath My commandments, and keepeth them, he it is that loveth Me: and he. . .shall be loved of My Father" (verse 14:21).

"If a man love Me, He will keep My words: and

My Father will love him" (verse 14:23).

"If ye abide in Me, and My words abide in you, ask what ye will, and it shall be done unto you" (15:7).

"If ye keep My commandments, ye shall abide in My love" (15:10).

"Ye are my friends, if ye do whatsoever I command you" (verse 15:14).

Study and compare these passages, until the words enter your heart and work the deep conviction that keeping Christ's commandments is the essential condition of all spiritual blessing. It is necessary for the coming of the Holy Spirit and His actual indwelling, for the enjoyment of the Father's love, and the manifestation of Christ in our life.

Power in prayer, the abiding in Christ's love, and the enjoyment of His friendship depends upon the keeping of the commandments. The power to claim and enjoy these blessings in faith day by day also requires obedience. The will of God, delighted in and done, is the only way to the heart of the Father and His only way to our heart. Keep the commandments: this is the way to every blessing.

Proving Our Love For Him

All this is confirmed by what we find in John's first epistle: "Hereby do we know that we know Him, if we keep His commandments. He that saith, I know Him, and keepeth not His commandments, is a liar. . . .But whoso keepeth His word, in him verily is the love of God perfected'' (1 John 2:3-5). The only proof of a true, living, saving knowledge of God; the only proof of not being self-deceived in our religion; the only proof of God's love not being an imagination, but a possession, is *keeping His Word*.

"If our heart condemns us not, then have we confidence toward God; and whatsoever we ask, we receive of Him, because we keep His commandments. . .And he that keepeth His commandments dwelleth in Him'' (1 John 3:21,22,24). Keeping the commandments is the secret of confidence toward God, and true intimate fellowship with Him.

"This is the love of God that we keep His commandments: for whatsoever is born of God overcometh the world'' (John 3:3,4). Our profession of love is worthless, unless it is proved to be true by the keeping of His commandments in the power of a life born of God. Knowing God, having the love of God perfected in us, having boldness with God, abiding in Him, being born of Him and loving Him—all is dependent upon one thing—*keeping the commandments* .

The Key To Blessing

When we realize the prominence Christ and Scripture give to keeping His commandments, we will learn to give it the same prominence in our life. It will become to us one of the keys to true Bible study. The person who reads his Bible with the determined purpose to search out and to obey every commandment of God and of Christ is on the right track to receiving all the blessing the Word was ever meant to bring. He will especially learn two things. First, he must wait for the teaching of the Holy Spirit to lead him into all God's will. Secondly, there is joy in performing daily duties because they are the will of God.

He will discover how all daily life is enriched when he says as Christ did: "This commandment have I received of My Father" (John 10:18). The Word will become the light and guide by which all his steps are ordered. His life will become the training school in which the power of the Word is proved and the mind is prepared to be taught and encouraged. The keeping of the commandments will be the key to every spiritual blessing.

Make a determined effort to understand what this life of full obedience means. Look at some of Christ's clearest commands: love one another even as I have loved you; ye ought to wash one another's feet; ye should do as I have done to you. Then accept Christlike love and humility as the law of the supernatural life you are to live. Let this thought encourage you to put your hope entirely in Him. By His Spirit, He will work in you both to will and to do that which pleases Him.

Once again, our one aim must be perfect harmony between conscience and conduct. Every conviction must be carried out into action. Christ's commands were meant to be obeyed. If this is not done, the accumulation of scriptural knowledge only hardens us and makes us unable to learn from the Spirit.

In your inner chamber each morning, you must decide whether you will keep the commandments of Christ throughout the day. This decision will also determine whether in future life you will be a person completely yielded to know and do the will of God.

Chapter 12

THE WORD IS LIFE

"And out of the ground made the Lord God to grow. . .the tree of life also in the midst of the garden, and the tree of knowledge of good and evil" —Genesis 2:9.

There are two ways of knowing things. The one is in the mind by thought or idea—I know about a thing. The other is by living—I know by experience. An intelligent blind man may know all that science teaches about the light by having books read to him. A child who has never thought about what light is knows more about light than the blind scholar. The scholar knows all about it by thinking. The child knows it in reality by seeing and enjoying it.

The Heart And The Life

This is also true in Christianity. The mind can form thoughts about God from the Bible and know all the doctrines of salvation, while the inner life does not know the power of God to save. This is why we read "He that loveth not knoweth not

God; for God is love'' (1 John 4:8). He may know all about God and love, he may be able to express beautiful thoughts about it, but unless he loves, he does not know God. Only love can know God. The knowledge of God is life eternal.

God's Word is the word of life. Out of the heart are the issues of life. The life of a person can be strong, even when mental knowledge is limited. On the other hand, knowledge can be the object of diligent study and great delight, while the person's life is not affected by it.

An illustration may make this plain. Suppose we could give understanding to an apple tree with eyes to see and hands to work. This might enable the apple tree to do for itself what the gardener does—to fertilize and water it. But the inner life of the apple tree would still be the same, quite different from the understanding given to it. And so the inner divine life of a person is something quite different from the intellect with which he knows about it. That intellect offers to the heart God's Word which the Holy Spirit can quicken. Yet, the intellect cannot impart or quicken the true life. It is only a servant that carries the food. It is the heart that must be nourished and live.

Knowledge Versus Life

The two trees in the garden are God's revelation of the same truth. If Adam had eaten of the tree of life, he would have received and known all the good God had for him in living power as an experience. And he would have known evil only by being absolutely free from it. Eve was led astray by the desire for knowledge—"a tree to be desired to make one wise" (Genesis 3:6). In this way, man got a knowledge of good without possessing it. He had a knowledge of good only from the evil that was its opposite. And since that day man has searched for truth more in knowledge than in life.

It is only by experiencing God and His goodness that we can receive true knowledge. The knowledge of the intellect cannot quicken. "Though I. . .understand all mysteries, and all knowledge. . .and have not charity (love), I am nothing" (1 Corinthians 13:2).

It is in our daily Bible reading that this danger must be met and conquered. We need the intellect to hear and understand God's Word in its human meaning. But we need to know that the possession of the truth by the intellect can only benefit us when the Holy Spirit makes it life and truth in the heart. We need to yield our heart and wait on God in quiet submission and faith to work in us by that Spirit. As this becomes a holy habit, our intellect and heart will work in perfect harmony. Each movement of the mind will be accompanied by the corresponding movement of the heart, waiting on and listening for the teaching of the Spirit.

Chapter 13

THE HEART AND THE INTELLECT

"Trust in the Lord with all thine heart; and lean not unto thine own understanding"—Proverbs 3:5.

The main purpose of the Book of Proverbs is to teach knowledge and discretion and to guide in the path of wisdom and understanding. To understand righteousness, to understand the fear of the Lord, to find good understanding—it is to these that Proverbs guides us. The writer of Proverbs warns us to distinguish between trusting our own understanding and seeking spiritual understanding which God gives.

"Trust in the Lord with all thine heart; and lean not unto thine own understanding." In all our seeking after knowledge and wisdom, in all our plans for our life or studying the Word, we have two powers at work: *the understanding* or intellect which knows things from the ideas we form; and *the heart* which knows them by experience as they become part of our will and desires.

Dangers Of The Intellect

One of the main reasons Bible teaching and Bible knowledge bear little fruit in the lives of Christians is because we trust to our own understanding.

Many people argue that God gave us our intellect, and without it there is no possibility of knowing God's Word. This is true, but in the fall our whole human nature was disordered. The will became enslaved, our affections were perverted, and our understanding was darkened. Everyone admits that even the believer does not have in himself the power of a holy will and needs the daily renewing of the grace of Jesus Christ. They admit that the believer does not have the power to love God and his neighbor unless it is given to him by the Holy Spirit. But most people do not realize that the intellect is equally ruined spiritually and incapable of understanding spiritual truth.

It was especially this desire for knowledge that led Eve astray and was the outcome of the temptation. To think that we can take the knowledge of God's truth for ourselves out of His Word is still our greatest danger. We need a deep conviction of the inability of our understanding to really know the truth. We need to realize the terrible danger of self-confidence and self-deception and to see the need for this warning: "Trust in the Lord with all thine heart, and lean not unto thine own understanding."

Look To Your Heart

It is with the heart man believes. It is with all the heart we are to seek, serve, and love God. It is only with the heart that we can know God or worship God in spirit and truth. It is in the heart, therefore, that the divine Word does the work. It is into our heart, God has sent forth the Spirit of His Son. It is the heart, the inward life of desire and love and will, that the Holy Spirit guides into all the truth.

The Bible says, "Trust in the Lord with all thine heart, and lean not unto thine own understanding." Do not trust your own understanding. It can only give you thoughts and ideas about spiritual things without the reality of them. It will deceive you with the thought that the truth, if received into the mind, will somehow surely enter your heart. It will blind you to the terrible experience which is universal: the practice of daily Bible reading, listening to God's Word every Sunday, and yet becoming neither humble, nor holy, nor heavenly minded because of it.

Instead of trusting your understanding, come with your heart to the Bible and trust Him. Let your whole heart be set upon the living God as the teacher when you enter your prayer closet. Then you will find good understanding. God will give you an understanding heart, a spiritual understanding.

You may ask, "But what am I to do? How am I to study my Bible? I see no way of doing so, unless I use my understanding."

That is correct, but do not use it for what it cannot do. Remember two things. One is that your understanding can only give you a picture or thought of spiritual things. The moment it has done this, go with your heart to the Lord to make His Word life and truth in you. The other danger of leaning to your own understanding is that you will take pride in your own intellect. Nothing can save you from this, except continual dependence of the heart on the Holy Spirit's teaching. When the Holy Spirit quickens the Word in the heart and affections, then He can guide the intellect. "The meek will He guide in judgment: and the meek will He teach His way" (Psalm 25:9). "The fear of the Lord is the beginning of wisdom" (Proverbs 9:10).

With every thought from the Word that your understanding grasps, bow before God in dependence and trust. Believe with your whole heart that God can and will make it true. Ask for the Holy Spirit to make it work in your heart until the Word becomes the strength of your life.

Persevere in this, and the time will come when the Holy Spirit, dwelling in the heart and life, will keep the understanding in subjection and let His holy light shine through it.

Chapter 14

GOD'S THOUGHTS AND OUR THOUGHTS

"As the heavens are higher than the earth, so are. . .my thoughts higher than your thoughts"—Isaiah 55:9.

On earth the words of a wise man often mean something different from what the hearer understands them to mean. How natural then that the words of God, as He understands them, mean something infinitely higher than we understand at first. We must remember this because it will cause us to search for the fuller meaning of God's Word as He meant it. It will give us confidence to hope that there is fulfillment in life beyond our highest thoughts.

God's Thoughts

God's Word has two meanings. The one is the meaning which originated in the mind of God, making human words the bearer of divine wisdom, power, and love. The other is our partial, distorted understanding of God's Word. Although such words as the love of God, the grace of God, and the power of God may seem very true and real to us, there is still an infinite fullness in the Word which we have not yet known. How strikingly this is put in our text from Isaiah—"As the heavens are higher than the earth." Our faith in this fact is so simple and clear that no one would dream of trying with his little arm to reach the sun or the stars. And now God says, "My thoughts are higher than your thoughts." Even when the Word has given us God's thoughts and our thoughts have tried to understand them, they still remain as high above our thoughts as the heavens are higher than the earth.

All the infinities of God and the eternal world dwell in the Word as the seed of eternal life. And just as the full-grown oak is so mysteriously greater than the acorn from which it sprang, so God's words are but seeds from which God's mighty wonders of grace and power can grow up.

A Childlike Spirit

We should learn to come to the Word as little children. Jesus said, "Thou hast hid these things from the wise and prudent, and hast revealed them unto babes" (Luke 10:21). The prudent and the wise are not necessarily hypocrites or enemies. There are many of God's own dear children, who, by neglecting to cultivate a childlike spirit, have spiritual truth hidden from them and never become spiritual men. "What man knoweth the things of a man, save the spirit of man which is in him? even so the things of God knoweth no man, but the Spirit of God. Now we have received...the spirit which is of God; that we might know'' (1 Corinthians 2:11,12). Let a deep sense of our ignorance, a deep distrust of our own power to understand the things of God influence our Bible study.

God wants to make His Word true in us. The Holy Spirit is already in us to reveal the things of God. In answer to our humble, believing prayer, God will give insight into the mystery of God— our wonderful union and likeness to Christ, His living in us, and our being as He was in this world.

If our hearts thirst, a time may come when, by a special communication of His Spirit, all our yearnings are satisfied. Christ will take possession of the heart and what was of faith now becomes an experience. Then we realize that, as the heavens are higher than the earth, His thoughts are higher than our thoughts.

Chapter 15

TRUE MEDITATION

"Blessed is the man. . .(whose) delight is in the law of the Lord; and in his law doth he meditate day and night"—Psalm 1:1,2.

"Let the words of my mouth, and the meditation of my heart, be acceptable in thy sight, O Lord"—Psalm 19:14.

The true aim of education, study, and reading is not what is brought into us, but what is brought out of ourselves, when we actually put into practice what we have learned. This is as true of the study of the Bible as of any other study. God's Word only works when the truth it brings to us has stirred the inner life and reproduced itself in trust, love, or adoration. When the heart has received the Word through the mind and has had its spiritual powers exercised, the Word is no longer void, but has done what God intended it to do. It has become part of our life and strengthened us for new purpose and effort.

The Art Of Meditation

It is in meditation that the heart holds and appropriates the Word. Just as in reflection our understanding grasps all meaning of a truth, so in meditation the heart assimilates it and makes truth a part of its own life. We must remember that the heart is the will and the affection. The meditation of the heart implies desire, acceptance, surrender, and love. Out of the heart are the issues of life. Whatever the heart truly believes, it receives and allows to master and rule the life. The intellect gathers and prepares the food on which we are to feed. In meditation the heart takes it in and feeds on it.

The art of meditation needs to be cultivated. Just as we need to be trained to concentrate our mental powers to think clearly, a Christian needs to meditate until he has formed the habit of yielding his whole heart to every word of God.

How can this power of meditation be cultivated? The very first thing we must do is present ourselves before God. It is His Word and it has no power of blessing apart from Him. The Word is meant to bring us into His presence and fellowship. Practice His presence. Take the Word as from God Himself with the assurance that He will make it work in your heart. In Psalm 119, the word meditate is mentioned seven times, each time as part of a prayer addressed to God: "I will meditate in Thy precepts" (verse 15); "Thy servant did meditate in Thy statutes" (verse 23). "O how I

66

love Thy law! it is my meditation all the day"
(verse 97). Meditation is turning our heart toward
God and seeking to make His Word a part of our
life.

Pondering In The Heart

Another element of true meditation is quiet
pondering. When we endeavor to master a teaching in Scripture, our intellect often needs to put
forth great effort. With meditation we must take a
different approach. Instead of striving, we must
hide the word we are studying in the depth of the
heart and believe that by the Holy Spirit its meaning and power will be revealed in our inner life.

"Thou desirest truth in the inward parts: and in
the hidden part Thou shalt make me to know wisdom" (Psalm 51:6). In the description of our
Lord's mother we are told: "Mary kept all these
things and pondered them in her heart" (Luke
2:19). Here we have a believer who has come to
know Christ and is on the sure way to knowing
Him better.

In meditation, personal application takes a
prominent place. This is not the case with our
intellectual study of the Bible: its object is to
know and understand. In meditation the chief purpose is to appropriate and experience. The true
spirit of Bible study is a readiness to believe every
promise implicitly and to obey every command
unhesitatingly. It is in quiet meditation that faith
is exercised, that full surrender to all God's will is
made, and the assurance of grace is received to

perform our vows.

Meditation And Prayer

Meditation must lead to prayer. It provides matter for prayer. It must lead on to prayer, to ask and receive definitely what it has seen in the Word or accepted in the Word. The value of meditation is that it prepares our hearts to pray about the needs the Word has revealed to us. The Word will open up and prove its power in the soul of the one who meekly and patiently waits for it.

There is reward in resting for a time from intellectual effort and cultivating the habit of holy meditation. In time the two will be brought into harmony, and our study will be enlightened by quiet waiting on God and a yielding of the heart and life to the Word.

We should have fellowship with God throughout the day. The habit of true meditation in the morning will bring us nearer the blessedness of the man of the first Psalm: "Blessed is the man. . .whose delight is in the law of the Lord; and in His law doth he meditate day and night" (1:1,2).

All Christian workers and leaders of God's people must remember that they need this time of meditation more than others. It will keep their own communication unbroken with their only source of strength and blessing. God says, "I will be with thee: I will not fail thee, nor forsake thee. . . .Only be thou strong and very courageous, that thou mayest observe to do according to all the law. . .that thou mayest prosper withersoever thou goest. This book of the law shall not depart out of thy mouth; but thou shalt meditate therein day and night. . .then thou shalt have good success. . .be strong and of a good courage'' (Joshua 1:5-9).

"Let the words of my mouth and the meditation of my heart be acceptable in Thy sight, O Lord, my strength, and my redeemer." Let this be your aim that your meditation may be acceptable in His sight—part of the spiritual sacrifice you offer. Let this be your prayer and expectation, that your meditation may be true worship—the living surrender of the heart to God's Word in His presence.

Chapter 16

HAVING A CHILDLIKE SPIRIT

"I thank thee, O Father, Lord of heaven and earth, because thou hast hid these things from the wise and prudent, and hast revealed them unto babes"—Matthew 11:25.

The wise and prudent are those who have confidence in their reasoning ability to help them in their pursuit of spiritual knowledge. The babes are those whose chief work is not the mind and its power, but the heart and its emotions. Ignorance, helplessness, dependence, meekness, teachableness, trust, and love—these are the qualities God seeks in those whom He teaches. (See Psalm 25:9,12,14,17,20.)

One of the most important parts of our devotions is the study of God's Word. In order to receive the Word in the Spirit, we must wait for the Father to reveal its truth in us. We must have that childlike attitude to which the Father loves to impart the secrets of His love. With the wise and prudent the most important thing is head knowledge. From them God hides the true spiritual meaning of the very thing they think they understand. With babes it is not the head and its knowledge, but the heart and its emotions that are important. Because they have a sense of humility, love, and trust, God reveals to them the very thing they know they cannot understand.

A Teachable Spirit

Education tells us that there are two styles of teaching. The ordinary teacher makes the communication of knowledge his main objective. He strives to cultivate the abilities of the child in order to help him attain this objective. The true teacher considers the amount of knowledge a secondary thing. His first aim is to develop the abilities of the child's mind and spirit. He helps the pupil, both mentally and morally, to use his abilities correctly in the pursuit and the application of knowledge.

Along the same line there are two classes of preachers. Some pour forth instruction, argument, and appeal and leave it to the hearers to make the best use they can of what is presented to them. The true preacher knows how much depends upon the condition of heart. He seeks, even as Jesus did, to make the teaching of objective truth or doctrine secondary to the cultivation of those attitudes without which teaching has little value.

A hundred eloquent sermons can be preached to wise and prudent Christians who listen with the idea that they can understand, and that what they hear will somehow profit them. However, if one

71

sermon is preached to hearers who are aware of their spiritual ignorance, they will receive the truth because of their childlike spirit. They will wait for and depend on the Father's teaching.

In the secret chamber every man is his own teacher and preacher. He is to train himself to have a childlike simplicity and a teachable spirit. He must remember that there must be an individual revelation of divine truth to each person by the Holy Spirit. He must wait on the Father to reveal to him, and within him, the hidden mystery in its power in the inner life. With this attitude he exercises the childlike spirit and receives the Kingdom as a little child.

All evangelical Christians believe in regeneration. However, few believe that when a man is born of God, his chief characteristic should be a childlike dependence on God for all teaching and strength. This was the one thing our Lord Jesus insisted on above all. He pronounced the poor in heart, the meek, the hungry, "blessed." He called men to learn that He was meek and lowly in heart. He spoke so often of humbling ourselves and becoming as little children. The first sign of being a child of God, of being like Jesus Christ, is an absolute dependence upon God for any real knowledge of spiritual things.

Revealed To Babes

Let each of us ask ourselves: Have I considered the childlike spirit essential for my Bible study? What use is Bible study without the childlike spirit? It is the only real key to God's school. We must set aside everything to attain this attitude. Only then will God reveal His hidden wisdom.

The new birth, being born of God, by which we become God's children, is intended to make us babes. It will give us the child-spirit as well as the child-teaching. It cannot do the second without the first. Let us yield ourselves to this new life in us, to the leading of the spirit. He will breathe in us the spirit of little children. The first objective of Bible study is to learn the hidden wisdom of God. The first condition of obtaining this knowledge is to accept the fact that God Himself reveals it to us.

In order to receive a revelation of God, we must first have this childlike spirit. We all know the first thing a wise workman does is to see that he has the proper tools and that they are in proper order. He does not consider it lost time to stop his work and sharpen the tools. It is not lost time to let the Bible study wait until you see whether you are in the right position—waiting for the Father's revelation with a meek and childlike spirit. If you feel that you have not read your Bible in this spirit, confess and forsake at once the self-confident spirit of the wise and prudent. Pray for the childlike spirit, and then believe you have it. Although it may be neglected and suppressed, it is in you. You can begin at once as a child of God to experience it.

This childlike spirit is in you, as a seed, in the new life, born of the Spirit. It must rise and grow in you as a birth of the indwelling Spirit. By faith you must pray for this grace of the Spirit and then exercise it. Live as a babe before God. As a new-born babe, desire the milk of the Word.

Beware of trying to assume this state of mind only when you want to study Scripture. It must be the permanent habit of your mind, the state of your heart. Then alone can you enjoy the continual guidance of the Holy Spirit.

Chapter 17

LEARNING OF CHRIST

"Take my yoke upon you and learn of me; for I am meek and lowly of heart: and ye shall find rest unto your souls"—Matthew 11:29.

All Bible study is learning. All Bible study in order to be fruitful should be learning of Christ. The Bible is the schoolbook, Christ is the teacher. It is He who opens the understanding, the heart, and the seals. (See Luke 24:45; Acts 16:14; Revelation 5:9.) Christ is the living eternal Word of which the written words are the human expression. Christ's presence and teaching are the secret of all true Bible study. The written Word is powerless, except as it brings us to the living Word.

No one has ever thought of accusing our Lord of not honoring the Old Testament. In His own life He proved that He loved it because it came out of the mouth of God. He always pointed the Jews to it as the revelation of God and the witness to Himself. But with the disciples it is remarkable how frequently He spoke of His own teaching as what they most needed and had to obey.

The Jews had their self-made interpretation of the Word and made it the greatest barrier between themselves and Him of whom it spoke. Christians often do this, too. Our human understanding of Scripture, fortified by the authority of the Church or our own denomination, becomes the greatest hindrance to Christ's teachings. Christ the living Word seeks first to find His place in our heart and life, to be our only teacher. From Him we will learn to honor and understand Scripture.

Learn To Be Meek

"Learn of Me for I am meek and lowly of heart." Our Lord gives us the secret of His own inner life which He brought down to us from heaven. This secret which He has given and which He wants us to learn from Him is found in the words, "I am meek and lowly of heart." It is the one virtue that makes Him the Lamb of God, our suffering Redeemer, our heavenly teacher and leader. It is the one attitude which He asks us to learn from Him—out of this all else will come.

For Bible study and all our Christian life this is the one condition we need to truly learn of Christ. He, the Teacher, meek and lowly of heart, wants to make you what He is, because that is salvation. As a learner you must come and study and believe in Him, the meek and lowly One. You must seek to learn of Him how to be meek and lowly, too.

Why is this the first and all-important requirement? Because it lies at the root of the true relationship of the believer to God. God alone has life and goodness and happiness. As the God of love, He delights to give and work these qualities into us. Christ became the Son of Man to show us how to live in complete dependence upon God. This is the meaning of His being lowly in heart.

Angels veil their faces and cast their crowns before God. God is everything to them. They delight to receive all and to give all. This is the root of the true Christian life: to be nothing before God and men; to wait on God alone; to delight in, to imitate, to learn of Christ, the meek and lowly One. This is the key to the teachings of Christ, the only key to the true knowledge of Scripture. It is in this character that Christ has come to teach: it is in this character alone that you can learn of Him.

Meekness And Bible Study

In the Christian Church there is a lack of humility and of the meek and lowly heart which was in the life of Christ and the teachings of God's Word. I am deeply persuaded that this lack lies at the root of ineffective and unfruitful work by the Church. It is only as we are meek and lowly in heart that Christ can teach us by His Spirit what God has for us.

Let each of us begin with ourselves and consider this as the first condition of discipleship, the first lesson the Master will teach us. Let us make all our Bible study a time of learning about Christ, trusting Him who is meek, gentle, and kind to work His own spirit and likeness in us. In due time our morning watch will be the scene of daily fellowship and daily blessing.

I know how difficult it is to expect that the meek and lowly heart should be the first consideration in Bible study. It is hard to make people realize that, in communion with God, our attitude and character means everything. A meek and lowly heart is the very seed and root of all Christian character. It is hard to convince us that without it Bible study is of very little value. The meek and lowly heart is possible because it is the very thing Christ offers to give, teaching us how to find and receive it in Himself. I urge all Bible students, thoughtfully and prayerfully, to make this the very first question to be settled in the inner chamber: Is my heart in the condition which my Teacher desires it to be? And if not, my first work is to yield myself to Him to work it in me.

Chapter 18

CHRIST YOUR TEACHER

"Take my yoke upon you and learn of me; for I am meek and lowly of heart: and ye shall find rest unto your souls"—Matthew 11:29.

The first virtue of a pupil is a willingness to be taught. What does this imply? He must have an awareness of his own ignorance, a readiness to give up his own way of thinking or doing. He must look at things from the teacher's standpoint. He must have a quiet confidence that the master knows and will show him how to learn to know, too. The meek and lowly spirit listens carefully to know what the teacher's will is and how to carry it out. If a pupil has this kind of spirit, it must be the teacher's fault if he does not learn.

Why is it that, with Christ as our teacher, there is so much failure and so little real growth in spiritual knowledge? Why is there so much hearing and reading of the Bible, so much profession of faith in it as our only rule of life, and yet such a lack of the manifestation of its spirit and its power? Why is there so much honest, earnest application in the prayer closet and in Bible study, but little of the joy and strength God's Word could give?

This question is one of extreme importance. There must be some reason why there are so many disciples of Jesus who think they honestly desire to know and do His will, and yet, by their own confession, they are not holding forth the Word of life as a light in the world. If the answer to this question could be found, their lives would be changed.

Learning From Christ

"Take My yoke upon you and learn of Me; for I am meek and lowly of heart and ye shall find rest unto your souls." Many have taken Christ as Savior but not as Teacher. They have put their trust in Him as the Good Shepherd who gave His life for the sheep, but they know little of the reality of His daily shepherding His flock, calling everyone by name, hearing His voice, or following Him alone. They know little about following the Lamb or receiving from Him the lamb nature. They seldom seek to be like Him, meek and lowly in heart.

It was by their three year course in His school that Christ's disciples were equipped for the baptism of the Holy Spirit and the fulfillment of all the wonderful promises He had given them. As we daily wait for, receive, and follow Christ's teaching, we can truly find rest to our souls. All the weariness and burden of strain, failure, and disappointment gives way to that divine peace which knows that all is being cared for by Christ Himself.

This teachable spirit that refuses to know or do anything in its own wisdom is to be the spirit of our whole life, every day and all day long. In the morning hour this spirit is to be cultivated, and deliverance from self is to be achieved. It is there, while occupied with the words of God, that we need daily to realize that these words have value only as they are opened up by the personal teaching of Christ. We daily need to experience that as the living Lord Jesus comes near and takes charge of us, His teaching can be received. It is during this quiet time that we must definitely ask and cultivate the teachable spirit that takes up His yoke and learns of Him.

It is said of the Holy Spirit who dwells in us, the Spirit of Christ Jesus, "He shall teach you all things" (John 14:26). If His whole life and work in us is a divine teaching, then we must have this teachable spirit within us. This will make our communion with God's Word and our daily life what our Lord Jesus can make it.

Unlearning And Humility

Unlearning is often the most important part of learning: wrong impressions, prejudices, and beliefs are obstacles in the way of learning. Until these have been removed, the teacher labors in vain. The knowledge he communicates only touches the surface. Deep under the surface, the pupil is guided by what has become second nature to him. The first work of the teacher is to discover,

81

to make the pupil see and remove these hindrances.

There can be no true and faithful learning about Christ when we are not ready to *unlearn*. By heredity, by education, by tradition, we have established our thoughts about religion and God's Word, which are often great hindrances to our learning the truth. To learn of Christ requires a willingness to subject every truth we hold to His inspection for criticism and correction.

Humility is the root virtue of the Christian life. The law is absolute in God's Kingdom—"He that shall humble himself shall be exalted" (Matthew 23:12). Our disappointment in striving after higher degrees of grace, faith, spiritual knowledge, and love depends upon this law. We have not accepted the humility of Christ as the beginning and the perfection of His salvation. "God giveth grace to the humble" (James 4:6) has a far wider and deeper application than we think.

In the morning watch we place ourselves as learners in Christ's school. Let humility be the distinguishing mark of the learner. Let us listen to the voice that says, "Take My yoke upon you and learn of Me; for I am meek and lowly of heart: And ye shall find rest to your souls."

Chapter 19

THE LIFE AND THE LIGHT

"In the beginning was the Word, and the Word was with God and the Word was God. In him was life; and the life was the light of men"—John 1:1,4.

"He that followeth me shall not walk in darkness, but shall have the light of life"—John 8:12.

Because Christ was God, He could be the Word of God. Because He had the life of the God in Himself, He could be the revealer of that life. And so, as the living Word, He is the life-giving Word. The written Word can be made void and of no effect when we trust human wisdom for an understanding of it. The written Word must be accepted as the seed in which the life of the living Word lies hidden. When it is quickened by the Holy Spirit, it can become to us the Word of life. Our communion with God's written Word must be inspired and regulated by faith in the eternal Word, who is God.

The Life Is Light

This same truth comes out in the expression that follows: the life is the light. When we see the light shining, we know that there is a source of that light in some form. This is also true in the spiritual world. There must be life before there can be light. There can be reflected light from a dead or dark object. There can be borrowed light without life. But true life can alone show true light. He that follows Christ will have the light of life.

These verses from John's gospel confirm what we learned about the Spirit of God. Even as Christ knows the things of God because He is the life of God, so Christ is the Word because He is God and has the life of God. So the light of God only shines where the life of God is. When the written Word brings us the life of the eternal Word, its light within the heart shines out into our life. Only as the Holy Spirit, who knows the things of God because He is the life of God, makes them life and truth within us, can our study of Scripture really bless us.

The one great lesson the Spirit seeks to enforce in regard to God's Word is this: only as Scripture is received out of the life of God into our life can there be any real knowledge of it. The Word is a seed that bears within it the divine life. When it is received in the good soil of a heart that hungers for that life, it will spring up and bring forth fruit like all seed, "after its kind." It will reproduce in our life the very life of God, the very likeness and character of the Father and the Son through the Holy Spirit.

Wait On The Lord

We want to apply these lessons in a practical way to our private Bible reading. The rules are very simple.

"Be still and know that I am God" (Psalm 46:10). Take time to be quiet and to be aware of God. "Hold thy peace at the presence of the Lord God" (Zephaniah 1:7). "Be silent before the Lord" (Zechariah 2:13). "The Lord is in His holy temple: let all the earth keep silence before Him" (Habakkuk 2:20). *Worship and wait on Him* that He may speak to you. Remember that *the Word comes out of the life,* the heart of God carrying His life to impart it to yours. It is nothing less than the life of God, so nothing less than the power of God can make it live in you.

Believe in Christ the living Word. "In Him was life; and the life was the light of men" (John 1:4). "He that followeth Me. . .shall have the light of life" (John 8:12). Follow Jesus in love and longing desire, in obedience and service, and His life will work in you—His life will be the light of your soul.

Ask the Father for the Holy Spirit to make the Word in your heart living and active. Hunger for the will of God as your daily food. Thirst for the living spring of the Spirit within you. Receive the Word into your will, your life, your joy—the life it brings will give the light with which it shines.

Understanding The Word

My own experience has taught me that it takes a long time before we clearly understand that the Word of God must be received into the life and not only in the mind. Even after we understand, it takes time before we fully believe and act on it. Study each lesson until you know it. The Word comes out of the life of God, carries that life in itself, seeks to enter my life and fill it with the life of God. This life is the light of men and gives the light of the knowledge of the glory of God.

You may find that this lesson takes more time than you think, that it hinders you more than it helps in your Bible study. Do not be afraid or impatient, but be assured that if you learn this lesson, you will realize that it has become a key you never had before to the hidden treasure of the Word, giving you true wisdom in the hidden part.

So I repeated again the simple words so blessed and true. The Spirit that lives in God alone knows the things of God. In the same way it is only the Spirit living in me that can make me know the things of God by imparting them to my life.

Christ was the Word because He was God and had the life of God. In the same way, the written Word can only bless me as Christ, the living Word, brings the life of God to me. The life of Christ is the light of men. Therefore, it is only as I have the life of Christ, through the Word, that I have the light of the knowledge of God.

Chapter 20

PRINCIPLES OF BIBLE STUDY

"Blessed is the man. . .(whose) delight is in the law of the Lord; and in his law doth he meditate day and night"—Psalm 1:1,2.

There is a desire in the Church for more Bible study. Evangelists like D.L. Moody and many others have proved what power there is in preaching drawn directly from God's Word and inspired by the faith of its power. Earnest Christians have asked: "Why can't our ministers speak in the same way, giving the very Word of God more emphasis?" Many young ministers have come away from seminary confessing that they were taught everything except the knowledge of how to study the Word or how to help others study it. In some of our churches, the desire has been expressed to supply this need in the training of ministers. Yet, it has been difficult for men with theological training to return to the simplicity and directness of God's Word. This simplicity is necessary in order to teach younger men the way to make Scripture the one source of their knowledge and teaching.

Bible study can bring a full blessing to individual lives by giving God's Word its true place in Christian work. Let us look at the principles underlying the demand for more Bible study and how it can be truly carried out.

God's Word Reveals God's Will

God's Word is the only authentic revelation of God's will. All human statements of divine truth, however correct, are defective and carry a measure of human authority. In the Word, the voice of God speaks to us directly. Every child of God is called to direct fellowship with the Father through the Word. God reveals His heart and grace in His Word. His child can receive from God all the life and power there is in the Word into his own heart and being.

We know how few secondhand reports of messages or events can be fully trusted. Very few men report accurately what they have heard. Every believer has the right and calling to stand in direct communication with God. God still reveals Himself to each individual in His Word.

This Word of God is a living Word. It carries a *divine quickening power* in it. The human expression of the truth is often an idea or image of the truth, appealing to the mind and having little or no effect on the person. Because it is God's own Word, His presence and power in it makes it effective. The words in which God has chosen to clothe His own divine thoughts are God-breathed, and the life of God dwells in them. God is not the God of the dead but of the living. The Word was inspired when first given, and the Spirit of God still breathes in it. God is still *in* and *with* His Word. Christians and teachers need to believe this. It will lead them to give the simple, divine Word a confidence that no human teaching can have.

The Interpreter Of The Word

Only God Himself can, and most surely will, be the interpreter of His Word. *Divine truth needs a divine teacher.* Spiritual understanding of spiritual things can only come from the Holy Spirit. The unique character of the Word is that it is essentially different from, and infinitely exalted above, all human understanding. The deeper our conviction of this fact, the more we will feel the need for supernatural, divine teaching. We will be brought to seek God Himself, and we will be led to find Him in the Holy Spirit who dwells in the heart. As we wait on and trust the Spirit, He will make us to know wisdom in the hidden part, in our heart and spirit. The Word prayerfully read and cherished in the heart by faith will, through the Spirit, be both light and life within us.

Unity of Will And Life

The Word brings us into the most intimate fellowship with God—unity of will and life. In the Word, God has revealed His whole heart and all His will. In His law and precepts, He tells us what He wants to do for us. As we accept that will in the Word as from God Himself and yield ourselves to its working, we learn to know God in His will. The Word works out His richest purpose as it fills us with the reverence and dependence that comes from the divine presence and nearness. Nothing less than this must be our aim and our experience in our study of the Bible.

In Holy Scripture we have the very words in which the Holy God has spoken and in which He speaks to us. These words are, today, full of the life of God. God is in them and makes His presence and power known to those who seek Him in them. To those who ask and wait for the teaching of the Holy Spirit who dwells within us, the Spirit will reveal the spiritual meaning and power of the Word. The Word is thus meant every day to be the means of the revelation of God Himself to the soul and of fellowship with Him.

Have we learned to apply these truths? The Word says: Seek God; hearken to God; wait for God; God will speak to you; let God teach you. All we hear about more Bible teaching and Bible study must lead to this one thing. We must be Christians in whom the Word is never separated from the living God Himself. We must live as Christians to whom God in heaven speaks every day and all day long.

Chapter 21

YOUR POSITION IN CHRIST

"Set your affection on things above. . .for ye are dead, and your life is hid with Christ in God"—Colossians 3:2,3.

When entering into God's presence in the morning hour, the Christian must realize who he is himself and where he stands in relation to God. Each person who claims access and an audience with the Most High must have a living sense of the place he has in Christ before God.

Who You Are

Who am I? Who is it that comes to ask God to meet me and spend the whole day with me? I am one who knows, by the Word and Spirit of God, that I am in Christ and that my life is hid with Christ in God. In Christ I died to sin and the world I am now taken out of them, separated from them, and delivered from their power. I have been raised together with Christ; and in Him, I live unto God. My life is hid with Christ in God. I can come to God to claim and obtain all the divine life that is hidden away in Him for today's need and supply.

Yes, this is who I am. I say it to God in humble, holy reverence. I say it to myself to encourage others, as well as myself, to seek and expect nothing less than grace to live the hidden life of heaven here on earth. I am one who longs to say, who does say, Christ is my life. The longing of my soul is for Christ, revealed by the Father Himself within the heart. Nothing less can satisfy me. My life is hid with Christ. He can be my life in no other way than as He is in my heart. I can be content with nothing less than Christ in my heart. Christ is the Savior from sin, the gift and instrument of God's love. Christ is my indwelling friend and Lord.

If God should ask, "Who are you?" I would reply, "I live in Christ and Christ in me. Lord, you alone can make me know and be all that truly means."

Living His Life

I come as one who desires, who seeks, to be prepared to live the life of Christ today on earth, to translate His hidden, heavenly glory into the language of daily life. As Christ lived on earth only to do the will of God, it is my great desire to stand perfect and complete in all His will. My ignorance of that will is very great. My power to do His will is even greater. And yet I come to God as one who must not compromise, as one who in all honesty accepts the high calling of living out fully the will of God in all things.

This desire brings me to the prayer closet. As I think of all my failures in fulfilling God's will, as I look ahead to all the temptations and dangers that await me, I can say to God—I come to claim the life hid in Christ, that I may live for Christ. I cannot be content without the quiet assurance that God will go with me and bless me.

Who am I that I should ask these great and wonderful things of God? Can I expect to live the life hid with Christ in God and manifest it in my mortal body? I can, because God Himself will work it in me by the Holy Spirit dwelling in me. The same God, who raised Christ from the dead and then set Him at His right hand, has raised me with Him and given me the Spirit of the glory of His Son in my heart. A life in Christ, given up to know and do all God's will, is the life God Himself will work and maintain increasingly in me by the Holy Spirit.

Presenting Myself To God

I come in the morning and present myself before Him to receive His hidden life so I can live it out in the flesh. I can wait confidently and quietly, as one in whom the Spirit dwells, for the Father to give the fresh anointing that teaches all things. I can wait for Him to take charge of the new day He has given me.

I am sure you realize how important the morning hour is to secure God's presence for the day. During that time you take a firm stand on the foundation of full redemption. Believe what God says to you. Accept what God has bestowed on you in Christ. Be what God has made you to be. Take time before God to confess your position in Christ. In a battle much depends upon an impregnable position. Take your place where God has placed you.

The very attempt to do this may at times interfere with your ordinary Bible study or prayer. That will be no loss. It will be fully recompensed later. Your life depends upon knowing who your God is and who you are as His redeemed one in Christ. Your daily Christian walk depends on this knowledge. When you have learned the secret, it will, even when you do not think of it, be the strength of your heart, both in going in before God and going out with Him to the world.

Chapter 22

THE WILL OF GOD

"Thy will be done in earth, as it is in heaven"—Matthew 6:10.

The will of God is the living power to which the world owes its existence. Through that will and according to that will, the world is what it is. The world is the manifestation or embodiment of that divine will in its wisdom, power and goodness. The world has, in beauty and glory, only what God has willed it to have. As His will formed the world, so His will upholds it every day. Creation does what it was destined for, it shows forth the glory of God. "Thou art worthy, O Lord, to receive glory. . .for Thou hast created all things, and for Thy pleasure they are and were created" (Revelation 4:11).

The *divine will* undertook the creation of a *human will* in His own image and likeness with the living power to know and cooperate with that *will* to which it owed its being. The unfallen angels consider it their highest honor and happiness to be able to will and do exactly what God wills and does. The glory of heaven is that God's will is done there. The sin and misery of fallen angels and men consists simply in their having turned away from and refused to do the will of God.

Restoring God's Will

Redemption is the restoration of God's will to its place in the world. To this end Christ came and showed, in a human life, how man has but *one thing to live for: to do the will of God*. He showed us how there was one way of conquering self-will—by a death to it, in obeying God's will even unto death. So He atoned for our self-will, conquered it for us, and opened a path through death and resurrection into a life entirely united to the will of God.

God's redeeming will is now able to do in fallen men what His creating will had done in nature. In Christ and His example, God has revealed the devotion to and the delight in His will which He asks and expects of us. In Christ and His Spirit, He renews and takes possession of our will. He works in it to make us able and willing to do all His will.

He Himself works all things after the counsel of His will. To "make you perfect in every good work to do His will, working in you that which is well-pleasing in His sight" (Hebrews 13:21). As this is revealed by the Holy Spirit, believed and received into the heart, we begin to acquire an insight into the prayer, "Thy will be done on earth as it is in heaven." Then the true desire is awakened in us for the life it promises.

It is essential to the believer that he realize his relationship to God's will and its claim on him. Many believers have no conception of what their faith or their feeling ought to be in regard to the will of God. How few say: My desire is to be in *complete harmony with the will of God*. I feel my one need is to maintain my surrender, to do what God wills me to do. By God's grace, every hour of my life can be lived in the will of God—doing His will as it is done in heaven.

Doing God's Will

As the divine will works out its purposes in us and masters the heart, we will have the courage to believe in the answer to the prayer our Lord taught us. Through Jesus Christ this working of God's will in us is carried out. It is close union to Him that gives the confidence that God will work everything in us. It is only this confidence in God, through Jesus Christ, that will assure us that we can do our part, and that our will on earth can correspond and cooperate with the will of God. Let this be the one thing our heart desires—that in everything the will of God be done in us and by us, as it is done in heaven.

The will of man cannot be disconnected from its living union with the Father here, nor the living presence of the Son. It is only by divine guidance, given through the Holy Spirit, that the will of God in its beauty and application to daily life can be truly known. This teaching will be given, not to the wise and prudent, but to those with a childlike attitude who are willing to wait for and depend on what is given them. Divine guidance will lead in the path of God's will.

Our secret communion with God is the place where we repeat and learn the great lessons concerning God's will.

The God whom I worship asks of me perfect union with His will. My worship means: "I delight to do Thy Will, O God." The morning hour, the inner chamber, the secret fellowship with God—these bring the knowledge of God's will and the power to perform it. As we surrender to do all God wills, our study of God's Word and our prayer time will bring true and full blessing.

Chapter 23

FEEDING ON THE WORD

"Thy words were found and I did eat them; and thy word was unto me the joy and rejoicing of mine heart"—Jeremiah 15:16.

This verse teaches us three things. First, it teaches that *the finding* of God's Word comes only to those who seek diligently for it. Secondly, *the eating* means the personal appropriation of the Word for our own sustenance, the taking up into our being the words of God. "Man shall not live by bread alone, but by every word that proceedeth out of the mouth of God" (Matthew 4:4). We also learn about *the rejoicing:* "The kingdom of heaven is like unto treasure hid in a field; the which when a man hath found, he hideth, and for joy thereof goeth and selleth all that he hath, and buyeth that field" (Matthew 13:44). In this verse we have the finding, the appropriating, and the rejoicing. "Thy words *were found*, and *I did eat* them, and Thy word was the *joy and rejoicing* of mine heart."

Finding And Eating

Eating is here the central thought. It is preceded by the searching and finding. It is accompanied and followed by the rejoicing. It is the only aim and use of the one; it is the only cause and life of the other. In the secrecy of the inner chamber much depends on this—*I did eat them!*

To realize the difference between this and the finding of God's words, compare the corn a man may have stored in his grainary with the bread he has on his table. All the diligent labor he has put into sowing and harvesting his grain cannot profit him unless he eats a daily portion of the bread his body requires. Do you see the application of this to your Scripture study in the morning quiet time? You need to *find* God's words, and by careful thought to master them, so as to have them stored in your mind and memory for your own use and that of others. In this work there may often be great joy, the joy of harvest or of victory—the joy of treasure secured or difficulties overcome. Yet, we must remember this finding and possessing the words of God is not the actual eating of them which alone brings divine life and strength to the soul.

The fact that a farmer possesses good, wholesome corn will not nourish him. The fact of being deeply interested in the knowledge of God's Word will not of itself nourish your soul. "Thy words were found"—that happened first. "And I did eat them"—that brought the joy and rejoicing.

Eating Every Day

What is this eating? The corn, which the farmer had grown and rejoiced in as his very own, could not nourish his life until he took it and ate it. He had to completely assimilate it, until it became part of himself, entering into his blood, forming his bones and flesh. This has to be done in a small quantity at a time, two or three times a day, every day of the year. This is the law of eating. It is not the amount of truth I gather from God's Word. It is not the interest or success of my Bible study. It is not the increased insight or understanding I am obtaining that brings health and growth to my spiritual life. Rather, this often leaves me very unspiritual with little of the holiness or humility of Christ Jesus. Something else is necessary in order for spiritual growth to take place.

Jesus said: "My meat is to do the will of Him that sent Me" (John 4:34). We must take a small portion of God's Word, some definite command or duty of the new life, and quietly receive it into our will and our heart. We must yield our whole being to its rule and vow in the power of the Lord Jesus to perform it. Then, we must go and do it—this is eating the Word. We take it into our inmost being until it becomes part of our very life. The same process must take place with a truth or a promise. What you have eaten becomes part of yourself, and you carry it with you wherever you go as part of the life you live.

The two points of difference between the corn

in the grainary and the bread on the table can apply to your study of the Bible. The gathering of Scripture knowledge is one thing. The eating of God's Word, the receiving it into your very heart by the power of the life-giving Spirit, is something very different. The two laws of eating the food, in contrast to those of finding it, must always be obeyed. You can gather and store grain to last for years. You cannot swallow a large enough quantity of bread to last for days. Day by day, and more than once a day, you take in your day's food. And so the eating of God's Word must be in small portions, only as much as the soul can receive and digest at one time. This must take place day by day, from one end of the year to the other.

It is such feeding on the Word which will enable me to say: "And Thy word was the joy and rejoicing of my heart." George Mueller said that he learned not to stop reading the Word until he felt happy in God. Then he felt prepared to go out and do his day's work.

Chapter 24

HOLIDAYS AND YOUR QUIET TIME

"If the goodman (master) of the house had known what hour the thief would come, he would have watched and not have suffered his house to be broken through"—Luke 12:39.

How leisure time is spent is a very important question since it greatly affects our character. It has been said that "Leisure hours are the hinge on which true education turns." It is true that developing a person's character is more important than training the mind and abilities. While a teacher can do much to stimulate and guide a student, every child has to work out his own character. It is in the leisure hours, when he is free from rules and observation, that a child shows what his true character is. This is the reason leisure time is considered all-important and all-powerful, the hinge on which true education turns. This statement can also be applied to Christianity.

The Problem With Vacations

At Bible college or school, students will take

103

time for their daily devotions as part of their regular routine. Their mind is geared for systematic work. They set aside time for devotions just as they do time for a class or private study.

When the time for vacation or a holiday comes and students are free to do exactly as they please, many find that the morning watch and fellowship with God interferes with their holiday pleasure. The holiday becomes the test of character, the proof of how one could say with Job, "I have esteemed the words of His mouth more than my necessary food" (Job 23:12). The question of how we spend our leisure time is very important. It is then that I turn freely and naturally to what I love most.

A teacher in a large school in America is reported to have said, "The greatest difficulty with which we have to contend is the summer vacation. Just when we have brought a child to a good point of discipline, and he responds to the best ideals, we lose him. When he comes back in the autumn, we have to begin and do it all over. The summer holiday simply demoralizes him."

This statement, referring to ordinary study and duty, is strong. Within certain limits it is applicable to the Christian life. The sudden relaxation of regular habits, and the subtle thought that perfect freedom to do as one likes means perfect happiness, causes many young students to backslide in their Christian walk. Older and more experienced Christians should help the younger ones to guard against this attitude. The attainment of months may be lost by the neglect of a week. We do not know what time the thief will come. The spirit of the morning watch means unceasing vigilance all day and every day.

Your Daily Duty

During vacation time or holidays the student is free from the rules under which he lives at school. But there are other laws: laws of morality and of health, from which there is no relaxation. The call to daily fellowship with God belongs not to the school rules but to the laws of duty. As much as we need every day during the holidays to eat and breathe, we need every day to eat the bread and breathe the air of heaven.

The morning watch, however, is not only a duty, but an unspeakable privilege and pleasure. Fellowship with God, abiding in Christ, loving the Word and meditating on it all day—these things are life and strength, health and gladness. Look upon them in this light. Believe in the power of the new nature within and act upon it. Although you do not feel the power, it will come true. Consider it a joy, and it will become a joy to you.

Above all, realize that the world needs you and depends on you to be its light. Christ is waiting for you as a member of His body, day by day, to do His saving work through you. Neither He, nor the world, nor you can afford to lose a single day. God has created and redeemed you, so that through you He may, as through the sun He lightens the world, let His light, life, and love shine out upon men. You need every day anew to be in communication with the fountain of all light.

Do not think of asking for a holiday from this communion with God. Cherish holidays for the special time it gives you to study beyond your ordinary Bible study course. Cherish your holidays for the special opportunity of more fellowship with the Father and the Son. Instead of holidays becoming a snare, make them a blessed time for victory over self and the world, of increase in grace and strength, of being blessed and made a blessing.

Chapter 25

YOUR INNER LIFE

"Ye fools, did not he that made that which is without make that which is within also"—Luke 11:40.

Every spirit seeks to create for itself a form or shape in which its life is embodied. The outward is the visible expression of the hidden, inward life. The outward is generally known before the inward. Through it the inward is developed and reaches its full perfection. The apostle Paul says, "Howbeit that was not first which is spiritual, but that which is natural; and afterward that which is spiritual" (1 Corinthians 15:46). To understand and maintain the right relationship between the inward and the outward is one of the greatest secrets of the Christian life.

If Adam in the garden had not listened to the serpent, his trial would have resulted in the perfecting of his inward life. The cause of all his misery and sin came when he gave himself to the power of the visible, outward world. Adam did not seek his happiness in the hidden, inward life of a heart in which God's command was honored. Instead, he fixed his desire on the world around him, on the pleasure that the knowledge of good and evil could give him.

The Life Within

All false religion, from the most degrading idolatry to the corruption of Judaism and Christianity, has its root in this desire. Deception takes place when the outward—that which pleases the eye, interests the mind, or gratifies the taste—takes the place of truth in the inward part, that hidden wisdom in the heart which God gives.

The New Testament reveals the importance of the inner life. The promise of the new covenant is: "I will put My law in their inward parts and write it in their hearts" (Jeremiah 31:33). "A new heart also will I give you, and a new spirit will I put within you. . .and I will put My Spirit within you" (Ezekiel 36:26, 27). The promise of our Lord Jesus was: "The Spirit of truth. . .shall be in you. . .At that day ye shall know that I am. . .in you" (John 14:17,20).

Christianity is a matter of the heart—a heart into which God has sent forth the Spirit of His Son, a heart in which the love of God is shed abroad and true salvation is found. The inner chamber, with its secret communion with the Father, who sees in secret, is the symbol and the training school for the inner life. The faithful, daily use of the inner chamber will make the inner, hidden life strong.

In religion the great danger is giving more time and interest to outward experiences than to inward reality. It is not the intensity of your Bible study, it is not the frequency or the fervency of your prayers or good works, that necessarily constitutes a true spiritual life. What we need to realize is that God is a Spirit. There is also a spirit within us who can know and receive Him and become conformed to His likeness. We can be a partaker of the very nature that characterizes Him as God in His goodness and love.

Your Hidden Treasure

Our salvation consists in the manifestation of the nature, life, and spirit of Christ Jesus in our outward and inward new man. This alone renews and regains the first life of God in the soul of man. Wherever you go, whatever you do, at home or at work, do all with a desire for union with Christ, in imitation of His character. Desire only that which increases the spirit and life of Christ in your soul. Desire to have all within you changed into the spirit of the holy Jesus.

Consider the treasure you have within you—the Savior of the world, the eternal Word of God. It is hidden in your heart as a seed of the divine nature, which overcomes sin and death within you and generates the life of heaven in your soul.

Look in your heart and your heart will find its Savior, its God, within itself. You see and feel nothing of God, because you seek for Him in books, in the church, in outward religious exercises. But you will not find Him there until you have first found Him in your heart. Seek for Him in your heart and you will never seek in vain, for He dwells there in His Holy Spirit!

Chapter 26

THE POWER FOR DAILY RENEWAL

"Though our outward man perish, yet the inward man is renewed day by day"—2 Corinthians 4:16.

"According to his mercy he saved us, by the washing of regeneration, and renewing of the Holy Ghost"—Titus 3:5

With every new day the life of nature is renewed. As the sun rises again with its light and warmth, the flowers open, the birds sing, and life is everywhere stirred and strengthened. As we rise from the rest of sleep and eat our morning food, we feel that we have gathered new strength for the duties of the day.

Our inner life needs daily renewal, too. It is only by fresh nourishment from God's Word and fresh communion with God Himself in prayer, that the vigor of the spiritual life can be maintained and grow. Our outward man may perish and the strain of work may exhaust us, yet the inner man can be renewed day by day.

Renewed By The Spirit

A quiet time and place with the Word and prayer are the means for daily renewal. To be effective, these means must be empowered by the Holy Spirit, the mighty power of God that works in us. In the text from Titus we are taught that we have been "saved by the washing of regeneration and renewing of the Holy Ghost." These two expressions are not meant to be a repetition. The regeneration is one great act, the beginning of the Christian life. The renewing of the Holy Spirit is a work that is carried on continuously and never ends.

In Romans 12:2, we read of the progressive transformation of the Christian life, that it is by "the renewing of the mind." In Ephesians 4:22, 23, while the words "put off the old man" indicate an act done once for all, the words "be renewed in the Spirit of your mind" are in the present tense and point to a progressive work. Even so in Colossians 3:10, we read, "ye have put on the new man, which is renewed in knowledge after the image of Him that created him." We can count on the blessed Spirit for the daily renewal of the inner man in the inner chamber.

In our private devotions, everything depends upon our maintaining the true relationship to the adorable third person of the blessed Trinity. It is only through the Holy Spirit that the Father and the Son can do their work of saving love, and through whom the Christian can do his work. That relationship may be expressed in two very simple words—faith and surrender.

Faith And Surrender

Faith. Scripture says, "God hath sent forth the Spirit of His Son into your hearts, crying, Abba, Father" (Galatians 4:6). The child of God, who in his morning devotion offers up prayer pleasing to the Father, must remember that he has received the Holy Spirit as the spirit of prayer. The Spirit's help is necessary to enable us to pray effectually. This is also true with the Word of God. It is by the Holy Spirit alone that the truth in its divine meaning and power can be revealed to us and do its work in our heart.

If the daily renewal of the inward man in the morning hour is to be a reality, take time to meditate, to worship, and to believe with your whole heart that the Holy Spirit has been given to you. Believe that He is within you and that through Him God will work the blessing which He gives through prayer and the Word.

Surrender. Do not forget that the Holy Spirit must have complete control. "As many as are led by the Spirit of God, they are the sons of God" (Romans 8:14). It is the ungrieved presence of the Spirit that can give the Word its light and keep us in that blessed life of childlike confidence and obedience which is pleasing to God. Let us praise God for this wonderful gift, the Holy Spirit in His renewing power. Let us look with new joy and hope to the inner chamber as the place where the inner man can indeed be renewed from day to day.

Our life will be kept fresh, and we will go on from strength to strength to bear much fruit, so that the Father may be glorified.

If all this is true, we need to know who the Holy Spirit is and what He does. As the third person of the Trinity, it is His work to bring the life of God to us, to hide Himself in the depth of our being and make Himself one with us. He is to reveal the Father and the Son, to be the mighty power of God working in us, and to take control of our entire being. He asks only one thing—simple obedience to His leading. The truly yielded soul will find in the daily renewing of the Holy Spirit the secret of growth, strength, and joy.

Chapter 27

RENEWED IN GOD'S IMAGE

"Seeing that ye have. . .put on the new man, which is renewed in knowledge after the image of him that created him"—Colossians 3:9,10.

"If so be that ye heard him, and have been taught by him. . .be renewed in the spirit of your mind; and that ye put on the new man, which after God is created in righteousness and true holiness"—Ephesians 4:21,23,24.

In every pursuit it is essential to have the goal clearly defined. It is not enough that there be movement and progress—we want to know that the movement is headed in the right direction. When we are in partnership with another person, on whom we are dependent, we need to know that our goal is the same. If our daily renewal is to attain its objective, we need to know clearly and hold firmly to what its purpose is.

"Ye have put on the new man, which is renewed in knowledge." The divine life, the work of the Holy Spirit within us, is no blind force. We are to be workers together with God. Our cooperation is to be intelligent and voluntary, "The new man is renewed day by day in knowledge." There is a knowledge which the natural understanding can draw from the Word, but which is without life and power. It has no real truth and substance which spiritual knowledge brings. It is the renewing of the Holy Spirit that gives true knowledge. This involves an inward tasting, a living experience of the very things of which the words are but the images. "The new man is renewed in knowledge." However diligent our Bible study may be, true knowledge is gained only as spiritual renewal is being experienced. Renewal in the spirit of the mind, in its life and inward being, can alone bring true divine knowledge.

Spiritual Renewal

What is the pattern that will be revealed to this spiritual knowledge which results from making renewal our only aim? "The new man is renewed in knowledge, after the image of Him that created him." The image, the likeness of God, is the one aim of the Holy Spirit in His daily renewing. That must also be the aim of the believer who seeks that renewing.

This was God's purpose in creation, "Let us make man in our image, after our likeness" (Genesis 1:26). God breathed His own life into man to reproduce in man a perfect likeness to God. In Christ, that image of God has been revealed and seen in human form. We have been predestined and redeemed and called. We are being taught and

116

equipped by the Holy Spirit to be conformed to the image of the Son, to be imitators of God, and to walk even as Christ walked. In order for daily renewal to take place and daily Bible study and prayer to be of value, we must set our heart on what God has set His on. We must desire that the new man be renewed day by day after the image of Him that created him.

Renewed In Righteousness And Holiness

In the passage from Ephesians, we have this same thought expressed somewhat differently. "Be renewed in the spirit of your mind, and put on the new man, which after God, according to the likeness of God, is created in righteousness and true holiness." *Righteousness* is God's hatred of sin and maintenance of the right. *Holiness* is God's glory, in the perfect harmony of His righteousness and love, His infinite exaltation above the creature, His perfect union with him.

Righteousness in man includes all God's will concerning our duty to Him and our fellowmen. Holiness involves our personal relationship to Himself. Just as the new man has been created, so it has to be daily renewed "after God in righteousness and holiness." The Holy Spirit is working in us to bring about this renewal. He waits for us day by day to yield ourselves to Him in His renewing grace and power.

The daily, returning morning hour is the time for daily renewing of the Holy Spirit into the image of God as righteousness and holiness. We need a time of meditation and prayer to get our heart set upon God's purposes. We need a true vision of how the inward man can be renewed day by day into the very likeness of God, changed into the same image by the Spirit of the Lord. Let nothing less be your aim or satisfy your aspirations. The image of God, the life of God, is in you, and His likeness can be seen in you. Do not separate yourself from God and His likeness. Let all our trust in Him mean nothing less than finding His likeness formed in you by the renewing of the Holy Spirit.

Let this be your daily prayer—to be renewed after the image of Him who created you.

Chapter 28

RENEWED AND TRANSFORMED

"For which cause we faint not; but though our outward man perish, yet the inward man is renewed day by day"—2 Corinthians 4:16.

"Be not conformed to this world: but be ye transformed by the renewing of your mind"—Romans 12:2.

It is not an easy thing to be a mature, strong Christian. It cost the Son of God His life. It is God's part to create a new man and to maintain that life with the unceasing daily care of the Holy Spirit.

When the new man is put on, it is our responsibility to see that the old man is put off. All the attitudes, habits, and pleasures of our own nature, that make up the life in which we have lived, are to be put away. All we have acquired by our natural birth from Adam is to be sold, if we are to possess the pearl of great price. If a man is to come after Christ, he must deny himself and take up his cross. He must forsake all and follow Christ in the path in which He walked. The Christian must cast away not only all sin, but everything, however legitimate and precious, that may cause him to sin. He is to hate his own life, to lose it, if he is to live in the power of eternal life. It is a serious thing, far more serious than most people think, to be a true Christian.

Renewing Your Mind

Paul speaks of the renewing of the inward man as being accompanied by the perishing of the outward man. The whole epistle of 2 Corinthians shows us how the fellowship of the sufferings of Christ, even in conformity to His death, was the secret of Paul's life of power and blessing to the churches. "Always bearing about in the body the dying of the Lord Jesus, that the life also of Jesus might be made manifest in our body. For we which live are alway delivered unto death for Jesus' sake, that the life also of Jesus might be manifested in our mortal flesh. So then death worketh in us, but life in you" (2 Corinthians 4:10-12).

The full experience of the life of Christ in our person, our body, and our work for others depends upon our fellowship in His suffering and death. There can be no large measure of the renewal of the inward man without the sacrifice, the perishing of the outward man.

To be filled with heaven, the life must be emptied of earth. We have the same truth in our second text, "Be ye transformed by the renewing of your mind." An old house may be renewed and yet keep very much of its old appearance. Or the renewal may be so complete that people exclaim, "What a transformation!" The renewing of the mind by the Holy Spirit means an entire transformation, an entirely different way of thinking, judging, deciding. The fleshly mind gives place to a "spiritual understanding" (see Colossians 1:9 and 1 John 5:20). This transformation is obtained only at the cost of giving up all that is of the old nature. "Be not conformed according to this world: but be ye transformed."

By nature we are of this world. When renewed by grace we are still in the world, subject to the subtle influence from which we cannot escape. The world is still in us, as the leaven of the nature which nothing can purge out except the mighty power of the Holy Spirit, who fills us with the life of heaven.

Being Transformed

Let us allow these truths to take hold and master us. The divine transformation, by the daily renewing of our mind into His image, can proceed in us only as we seek to be freed from every conformity to this world. The negative, "Be not conformed to this world," needs to be emphasized as strongly as the positive, "be ye transformed." The spirit of this world and the Spirit of God contend for the possession of our being.

Only as the spirit of this world is recognized, renounced, and cast out can the heavenly Spirit enter in. Then the Holy Spirit can do His blessed work of renewing and transforming. The world and whatever is of the worldly spirit must be given up. Our life and whatever is of self must be lost. This daily renewal of the inward man is very costly if we are trying to do it in our own strength. When we really learn that the Holy Spirit does everything, and by faith give up the struggle, the renewing becomes the simple, natural, healthy, joyful growth of the heavenly life in us.

The inner chamber then becomes the place we long for every day to praise God for what He has done, is doing, and what we know He will do. Day by day, we yield ourselves afresh to the blessed Lord who has said, "He that believeth on Me. . .out of his belly shall flow rivers of living water" (John 7:38). "The renewing of the Holy Ghost" becomes one of the most blessed truths of our daily Christian life.

Chapter 29

TO BE MADE HOLY

"Sanctify them through thy truth: thy word is truth"—John 17:17.

In His great intercessory prayer, our Lord spoke of the words which the Father had given Him, of giving them Himself to His disciples, and of their having received and believed them. It was this that made them disciples. It was their keeping these words that would really enable them to live the life and do the work of true disciples. Receiving the words of God from Christ and keeping them are the signs and power of true discipleship.

When praying to the Father, our Lord asks that He sanctify the disciples in the truth, as it dwells and works in His Word. Christ has said of Himself, "I am the truth" (John 14:6). He was the only begotten of the Father, full of grace and truth. His teaching was not like that of the law which came by Moses. Jesus' words were more than a promise of good things to come. "The words that I speak unto you, they are spirit, and they are life" (John 6:63). Christ had spoken of the Spirit of truth who would lead into all the truth in Himself, not a matter of knowledge or doctrine, but into its actual experience and enjoyment.

He prays that in this living truth the Father would sanctify them. "For their sakes," He says, "I sanctify Myself, that they also might be sanctified through the truth" (John 17:19). He asks the Father in His power and love to take charge of them, that His objective—to sanctify them in the truth, through His Word which is truth—might be realized. His desire is that they, like Himself, may be sanctified in truth. Let us study the wonderful lessons given in this verse in regard to God's Word.

The Word Makes Holy

"Sanctify them through Thy truth: Thy word is truth." The great objective of God's Word is to make us holy. No diligence or success in Bible study will really profit us unless it makes us more humble and holy. In our use of Holy Scripture this must be our main objective. The reason there is often so much Bible reading with so little real result in a Christlike character is that "salvation, through sanctification of the Spirit and belief of the truth" (2 Thessalonians 2:13) is not truly desired.

People imagine that if they study the Word and accept its truths, this will in some way benefit them. But experience teaches that it does not. The fruit of holy character, of consecrated life, of power to bless others, does not come for the simple reason that we only get what we seek. Christ gave us God's Word to make us holy. When we make this our definite aim in all Bible study, the truth, not the doctrinal truth, but its divine quickening power, can impart the very life of God to us.

"Sanctify them through Thy truth: Thy word is truth." It is God Himself who alone can make us holy by His Word. The Word, separate from God and His direct operation, cannot accomplish anything in us. The Word is an instrument: God Himself must use it. God is the only holy One. He alone can make holy. The unspeakable value of God's Word is that it is God's means of holiness. The terrible mistake of many people is that they forget that God alone can use it and make it effective.

It is not enough that I have access to the office of a physician. I need for him to prescribe a cure. Without him my use of his medicines could be fatal. This was true of the scribes and Pharisees of Jesus' day. They made their boast in God's law. They delighted in their study of Scripture and yet remained unsanctified. The Word did not sanctify them, because they did not seek for this in the Word and did not yield to God to do it for them.

God Makes Holy

"Sanctify them through Thy truth: Thy word is truth." This holiness through the Word must be sought and waited for from God in prayer. Our Lord taught His disciples that they must be holy. He sanctified Himself for them, that they might be sanctified in truth. He also brought His words and His work to the Father with the prayer that He would sanctify them. It is necessary to know God's Word and meditate on it. It is necessary to set our heart upon being holy and make this our primary objective in studying the Word. But all this is not enough. Everything depends upon our asking the Father to sanctify us through the Word. It is God, the holy Father, who makes us holy by the Spirit of holiness who dwells within us. He works in us the very mind and attitudes of Christ who is our sanctification.

"There is none holy as the Lord" (1 Samuel 2:2). All holiness is His, and He makes things holy by His holy presence. The tabernacle and temple were not holy in virtue of cleansing, separation, or consecration. They became holy by the incoming and indwelling God. His taking possession made them holy. God makes us holy through His Word bringing Christ and the Holy Spirit into us. The Father can only do this as we wait before Him and in deep dependence and full surrender give ourselves up to Him. When we pray by faith, "Sanctify me through Thy truth; Thy word is truth," our knowledge of God's Word will truly make us holy.

The morning watch is a sacred time. It is the time especially devoted to the yielding of ourselves to God's holiness, to be sanctified through the Word. Let us remember, the one aim of God's Word is to make us holy. Let this be our continual prayer, "Father, sanctify me through Thy truth."

Chapter 30

TEACHINGS FROM PSALM 119

"Oh how love I thy law! it is my meditation all the day. Consider how I love thy precepts. I love them exceedingly"—Psalm 119:97,159,167.

In Holy Scripture there is one portion devoted to teaching us the place which God's Word should have in our lives. It is the longest chapter in the Bible, and in almost every one of its 176 verses the Word is mentioned, using different names. Anyone who really wants to know how to study his Bible according to God's will should make a careful study of this psalm.

There should come a time in your life when you resolve to study its teaching and carry it out into practice. It is no wonder that our Bible study does not bring us more spiritual profit and strength, if we neglect the *divine directory* given to us in this psalm. It is possible you have never read it once through as a whole. Take time to read it through and understand its main ideas. If you find it difficult to do this by reading it once, read it more than once. This will make you feel the need to give it more careful thought.

Studying Psalm 119

The following hints may help you in studying this psalm.

Take note of all the *different names* which refer to God's Word. Then take note of all the *different verbs* expressing how we should feel and what we should do in regard to the Word. Let this lead you to consider carefully the place God's Word claims in your heart and life. Consider how every faculty of your being—desire, love, joy, trust, obedience, and action—is summoned by God's Word.

Count how many times the writer speaks in the past tense of his having kept, observed, and delighted in God's testimonies. Notice how many times he expresses in the present tense how he rejoices in, loves, and esteems God's law. Consider how, in the future tense, he promises and vows to observe God's precepts to the end. Put all these together and see how more than a hundred times he presents himself before God as *one who honors and keeps His law* . Study this, especially as these expressions are connected with his prayers to God until you have a clear image of the righteous man whose fervent, effectual prayer avails much.

Study *the prayers* themselves and note the different requests he makes with regard to the Word. The psalmist asks for understanding and the power to observe it. He prays to receive the blessing promised in the Word and to be found actually doing it. Note especially prayers like "teach me Thy statutes," and "give me understanding." Also study those where the plea is "according to Thy Word."

Count the verses in which there is any reference to *affliction* from his own sinful condition, from his enemies, from the sins of the wicked, or God delaying "to help him." Learn how it is in the time of trouble that we need God's Word especially and that this alone can bring comfort to us.

The Word And Fellowship With God

Notice how often the little pronouns Thou, Thine, Thee, occur and how often they are understood in every petition: "teach Thou me," "quicken Thou me," Then you will see how the whole psalm is a prayer spoken to God. All the psalmist has to say about the Word of God, with regard to his own attachment to it and his need for God's teaching, is spoken into the face of God. He believes that it is pleasing to God and good for his own soul to connect his meditation on the Word by prayer with the living God Himself. Every thought of God's Word, instead of drawing him away from God, leads him to fellowship with God.

The Word of God becomes to him the rich and inexhaustible material for having communion with God. As we gradually get an insight into these truths we will get new meaning from the individual verses. When we take a whole paragraph with its eight verses, we will find how they help to lift us into God's presence. We will be lifted into that life of obedience and joy which says, "I have sworn, and will perform it, that I will keep Thy righteous judgments" (Psalm 119:106). "Oh how I love Thy law; it is my meditation all the day."

Let us seek by the grace of the Holy Spirit to have the kind of devotional life which this psalm reveals. Let God's Word every day, and before everything else, lead us to God. Let every blessing in it be a matter of prayer, especially our need for divine teaching. Let our intense attachment to it be our childlike plea and confidence that the Father will help us. Let our prayers be followed by the vow that as God quickens and blesses us, we will obey His commandments. Let all that God's Word brings to us make us more earnest in longing to carry that Word to others.

Chapter 31

THE TRINITY AND YOU

"For this cause I bow my knees to the Father. . .that he would grant you, to be strengthened with might by his Spirit in the inner man; that Christ may dwell in your hearts by faith; that ye, being rooted and grounded in love, may be able. . .to know the love of Christ, which passeth knowledge, that ye might be filled with all the fullness of God. Now unto him that is able to do exceeding abundantly above all that we ask or think, according to the power that worketh in us, (the Holy Spirit), unto him be glory in the church by Christ Jesus throughout all ages. Amen"—Ephesians 3:14-21.

These words have often been regarded as one of the highest expressions of what the life of a believer may be on earth. Yet, this view is not without its dangers, if it fosters the idea that the attainment of such an experience is something exceptional and distant. Rather, this truth is meant to be the certain and immediate inheritance of every child of God.

Every morning each believer has the right to say: My Father will strengthen me today with power, is strengthening me even now in the inner man through His Spirit. Each day we are to be content with nothing less than the indwelling of Christ by faith, a life rooted in love, and made strong to know the love of Christ. Each day we must believe that the blessed work of being filled with all the fullness of God is being accomplished in us. Each day we must be strong in the faith of God's power and be giving Him glory in Christ. We must believe He is able to do above what we ask and think, according to the power of the Spirit working in us.

The Trinity In Daily Life

The text from Ephesians presents the truth of the Holy Trinity in relation to our practical life. Many Christians understand that it is necessary at different times in the Christian life to give special attention to the three persons of the blessed Trinity. They often feel it difficult to combine the various truths into one and to know how to worship the three in one. Our text reveals this wonderful relationship and the perfect unity.

We have the Spirit within us as the power of God, and yet He does not work according to our will or His own. It is the Father who grants us to be strengthened "through the Spirit in the inner man." It is the Father who does exceeding abundantly above all we ask or think "according to the power that worketh in us." The Spirit within us makes us more dependent on the Father. The Spirit can only work as the Father works through Him. We need to combine trusting awareness of the Holy Spirit indwelling us with a dependent waiting on the Father to work through Him.

This combined work is also necessary in our relationship with Christ. We bow our knees to God as Father in the name of the Son. We ask Him to strengthen us through the Spirit so that Christ may dwell in our heart. The Son leads to the Father and the Father again reveals the Son in us. Then, as the Son dwells in the heart and is rooted and grounded in love, we are led on to be filled with all the fullness of God. Our heart becomes the scene of the interchange of the operation of the Holy Three. As our hearts believe this, we give glory through Christ to Him who is able to do more than we can think by His Holy Spirit.

Our heart becomes the scene of a wonderful performance: *the Father* breathing His Spirit into us and making our heart the home of Christ; the *Holy Spirit* revealing and forming Christ within us, so that His very nature and character become ours; *the Son* imparting His life of love and leading us on to be filled with all the fullness of God.

Let us worship the three-in-one God in the fullness of faith every day. In whatever direction our Bible study and our prayer lead us, let this ever be the center from which we go out and to which we return. We were created in the image of the three-in-one God. The salvation by which God restores us is an inward salvation of our heart. The God who saves us can do it in no other way than as the indwelling God, filling us with all His fullness. Let us worship and wait. Let us believe and give Him glory.

The Trinity In Ephesians

Have you ever noticed in Ephesians how the three persons of the Trinity are always mentioned together.

1:3.	The Father, Jesus Christ, spiritual (or Holy Ghost) blessings.
1:12,13.	The Father, to the praise of His Glory, in Christ, sealed with the Holy Spirit.
1:17.	The Father, our Lord Jesus, the Spirit of Wisdom.
2:18.	Access through Christ, by one Spirit, to the Father.
2:22.	In Christ, an habitation of God, through the Spirit.
3:4-9.	The mystery of Christ, hid in God, preached by the Grace of God, revealed by the Spirit.
4:4-6.	One Spirit, one Lord, one God and Father.
5:18-20.	Filled with the Spirit, giving thanks to God, in the name of Christ.
6:10-18.	Strong in the Lord, the whole armour of God, the sword of the Spirit, praying in the Spirit.

As you study and compare these passages, notice especially how practical this truth of the Holy

Trinity is. Scripture teaches little about its mystery in the divine nature, but refers only to God's work in us and our faith and experience of His salvation.

True faith in the Trinity will make us strong, alert, God-possessed Christians. The divine *Spirit* will make Himself one with our life and inner being. The Blessed *Son* will dwell in us, as the way to perfect fellowship with God. The *Father*, through the Spirit and the Son, will work His purpose so that we are filled with all the fullness of God.

Let us bow our knees unto the Father! Then the mystery of the Trinity will be known and experienced.

Chapter 32

ABIDING IN CHRIST

"Abide in me, and I in you"—John 15:4.

When some knowledge has been obtained in words or deeds, in nature or history, the mind is prepared to seek for the inner meaning hidden in them. This is true with the teaching of Scripture concerning Jesus Christ. He is set before us as a man among us, before us, above us, doing a work for us here on earth and continuing that work for us in heaven. Many Christians never advance beyond an external exalted Lord, in whom they trust for what He has done and is doing for them and in them. They know and enjoy little of the power of the true mystery of Christ in us, of His inward presence, as an indwelling Savior.

The former and simpler view is that of the first three gospels. The more advanced view is found in the gospel of John. The former is the aspect of truth presented in the doctrine of justification. The latter is the teaching concerning the union of the believer with Christ and his continual abiding as taught in John and the epistles to the Ephesians and Colossians.

Abiding In Christ

This abiding in Christ and Christ in you must be more than a truth you hold in its right place in your scheme of gospel doctrine. It must be a matter of life and experience that inspires your faith in Christ and relationship with God. To be in a room means to have all that there is in it at your disposal, its furniture, its comforts, its light, its air, its shelter. To be in Christ, to abide in Christ, is not a matter of intellectual faith, but a spiritual reality.

Think who and what Christ is. Consider Him in the five stages that reveal His nature and work. He is *the incarnate One*, in whom we see God's omnipotence united perfectly in the divine and human nature. Living in Him we are partaking of the divine nature and of eternal life. He is *the obedient One*, living a life of entire surrender to God and perfect dependence on Him. Living in Him our life becomes one of complete subjection to God's will and continual waiting upon His guidance. He is *the crucified One*, who died for sin and to sin that He might take it away. Living in Him we are free from its curse and dominion. We live, like Him, in death to the world and our own will. He is *the risen One*, who lives forever. Living in Him we share His resurrection power and walk in newness of life, a life that has triumphed over sin and death. He is the exalted One, sitting on the throne and carrying on His work for the salvation of men. Living in Him His love possesses us, and we give ourselves to Him to be used in winning the world back to God.

Being in Christ, abiding in Him, means the soul is placed by God Himself in the midst of this wonderful environment of the life of Christ. We are given up to God, in obedience and sacrifice, filled with God in resurrection life and glory. The nature and character of Jesus Christ—His attitudes and affections, His power and glory—these are the elements in which we live, the air we breathe, the life in which our life exists and grows.

The Indwelling Christ

The full manifestations of God and His saving love can come in no other way than by indwelling. In virtue of Christ's divinity and divine power, He can, as we abide in Him, dwell in us. To the degree our heart is given to Him in faith and our will is given in active obedience, He comes in and abides in us. We can say, because we know: Christ liveth in me.

If we are to actually live with Christ in us and we in Him, then we must be renewed and strengthened in our personal relationship with God in the morning watch. Our access to God, our sacrifice to God, our expectation from God, must all be in Christ, in living fellowship with Him. If you feel that you want to get nearer to God, to realize His presence or power more fully—come to God in Christ. Think how Jesus, a man on earth, drew near to the Father in deep humility and dependence, in full surrender and entire obedience. We must come in His spirit and character, in union with Jesus.

Seek to take the very place before God that Christ has taken in heaven, that of an accomplished redemption, of a perfect victory, of full entrance to God's glory. Take the very place before God that Christ took on earth on His way to the victory and the glory. Do it by faith in His indwelling and enabling power in you here on earth. Expect your approach to God to be accepted, not according to your attainment, but according to your heart's surrender and your acceptance in Christ. Then you will be led on in the path in which Christ, living in you and speaking in you, will be truth and power.

Chapter 33

THE JOY OF BEING ALONE

"When Jesus therefore perceived that they would come and take him by force to make him a king, he departed again into a mountain himself alone"—John 6:15.

The gospels frequently tell us of Christ's going into solitude for prayer. Luke mentioned Christ's praying eleven times. Mark tells us in his very first chapter, that after a busy evening of healing many people, "in the morning rising up a great while before day, He went out, and departed into a solitary place and there prayed" (Mark 1:35). Before He chose His twelve apostles "He went out into a mountain to pray, and continued all night in prayer to God" (Luke 6:12). This thought of complete retreat from others appears to have deeply impressed the disciples. John uses the significant expression, "He departed into a mountain *Himself alone.*" Matthew also had written, "He went up into a mountain apart to pray: and when the evening was come, He was there alone" (Matthew 14:23). The man Christ Jesus felt the need for perfect solitude. Let us humbly seek to find out what this means.

Alone By Himself

Jesus went entirely by Himself, alone with Himself. Relationships with people can draw us away from ourselves and exhaust our energies. The man Christ Jesus knew this and felt the need to come apart by Himself. He needed to renew the consciousness of who He was and to realize His high destiny, His human weakness, His entire dependence on the Father.

How much more does the child of God need to come apart by himself. It may be for the maintenance of our own Christian life, or the renewal of our power to influence men for God, but whatever the reason there is an urgent call to every believer to follow in His Master's steps. We must find the place and the time where we can indeed be alone with God.

Alone With Spiritual Realities

When we withdraw completely from contact with temporal things, we are free to yield ourselves to the powers of the unseen world. Jesus needed quiet time to realize the power of the kingdom of darkness with which He had come to contend and to conquer. He needed a fresh awareness of the needs of this great world of mankind which He had come to save. He needed to be reminded of the presence and the power of the Father whose will He had come to do.

It is essential for a person in Christian service to set himself apart to think intensely on the spiritual realities with which he is so familiar, yet which often exercise so little power on his heart and life. The truths of eternity have an infinite power. They are often powerless because we do not give them time to reveal themselves. Taking time to be alone with God is the only remedy.

Alone With The Father

It is sometimes said that work is worship, that service is fellowship. If ever there were a man who could dispense with special seasons for solitude and fellowship, it was our blessed Lord. But He could not do His work or maintain His fellowship in full power without His quiet time. As a man He felt the need to bring all His work, past and future, and present it before the Father. He needed to renew His sense of absolute dependence on the Father's power and His absolute confidence in the Father's love in seasons of special fellowship. When He said: "the Son can do nothing of Himself," "as I hear so I speak," He was but expressing the simple truth of His relationship to God. It was this relationship that made His going apart a necessity and an unspeakable joy.

Every servant of His should understand and practice this blessed art of coming apart with God. The Church should train its children to exercise this high and holy privilege. Every believer may and must have his time when he is alone with God. It is a blessed experience to have God all alone to myself and to know that God has me all alone to Himself.

Alone With The Word And Prayer

Jesus had to learn God's Word as a child. During the long years of His life in Nazareth, He fed on that Word and made it His own. In His solitude He conferred with the Father on all the Word spoke of Him, on all the will of God it revealed for Him to do.

One of the deepest lessons a Christian has to learn is that the Word without the living God is of little value. The blessing of the Word comes when it brings us to the living God. The Word that we get from the mouth of God brings the power to know it and to do it. Let us learn this lesson: personal fellowship with God alone in secret can make the Word alive and powerful.

Prayer allows a person to lay open his whole life to God and to ask for His teaching and His strength. Just try for a moment to think what prayer meant to Jesus, what adoring worship, what humble love, what childlike pleading for all He needed. This must make us realize the joy that awaits the person who knows to follow in Christ's steps. God can do great things through the one who makes being alone with God his chief joy in life.

"Himself alone"—these words reveal to us the secret of the life of Christ on earth and of the life that He now lives in us. One of the most blessed elements of our life in the Holy Spirit is that He

reveals and imparts to us all that it means to be—Himself alone.

Chapter 34

THE POWER OF INTERCESSION

"Tell me, I pray thee, wherein thy great strength lieth"—Judges 16:6.

This is the question we would like to ask the men who, as intercessors for others, have had power with God and have prevailed. More than one Christian who has desired to give himself to this ministry has wondered why he has found it so difficult to rejoice in it, to persevere, and to prevail. Let us study the lives of the leaders and heroes of the prayer world. Maybe some of the elements of their success will be revealed to us.

The true intercessor is a person who knows that his heart and life are wholly given up to God and His glory. This is the only condition on which an officer at the court of an earthly king could expect to exert much influence. Moses, Elijah, Daniel and Paul prove that this is true in the spiritual world. Our blessed Lord is Himself the proof of it. He did not save us by intercession, but by self sacrifice. His power of intercession has its roots in His sacrifice: it claims and receives what the sacrifice won.

"He poured out His soul unto death: and He was numbered with the transgressors; and He bare the sins of many and made intercession for the transgressors" (Isaiah 53:12). He first gave Himself up to the will of God. There He won the power to influence and guide that will. Because He gave Himself for sinners in all-consuming love, He won the power to intercede for them.

You Can Intercede

The Christian, who seeks to enter personally into death with Christ and gives himself for God and others, will dare to be bold like Moses and Elijah, will persevere like Daniel or Paul. Wholehearted devotion and obedience to God are the characteristics of an intercessor.

You can complain that you are not able to pray like a true intercessor and ask how you can be equipped to do so. You talk about the weakness of your faith in God, your lack of love for souls, and your lack of delight in prayer. The man who is to have power in intercession must stop these complaints. He must confess that he has a nature perfectly adapted to the work God has called him to do. An apple tree is only expected to bear apples, because it has the apple nature within it. "You are God's workmanship, created in Christ Jesus unto good works" (Ephesians 2:10). The eye was created to see, and it is beautifully equipped for its work!

You are created in Christ to pray. It is your very nature as a child of God. Why do you think the

146

Spirit has been sent into your heart? To cry Abba, Father, to draw your heart up in childlike prayer. The Holy Spirit prays in us with groanings that cannot be uttered, with a divine power which our mind and feelings cannot understand. If you want to be an intercessor, give the Holy Spirit much greater honor than He usually receives. Believe that He is praying within you, and then be strong and of good courage. As you pray, be still before God to believe and yield to this wonderful power of prayer within you.

Power To Intercede

You have learned to *pray in the name of Christ*. This name means living power. You are in Christ, and He is in you. Your whole life is hidden and united with His, and His whole life is hidden and working in you. The Christian who is to intercede in power must clearly understand that he and Christ are one in the work of intercession. He appears before God clothed with the name and the nature, the righteousness and worthiness, the image, spirit, and life of Christ.

Do not spend your time in prayer repeating your petition, but humbly and confidently claim your place in Christ, your perfect union with Him, your access to God in Him. The believer, who comes to God in Christ as his life and trust, will have power to intercede.

Intercession is primarily a *work of faith*. It requires faith that believes the prayer will be heard, as well as faith that is comfortable with heavenly realities. We must have faith that does not worry about one's own unworthiness, because he is living in Christ. Intercession requires faith that does not depend upon its feelings, but upon the faithfulness of God. We need faith that has overcome the world and sacrifices the visible to be free for the spiritual to take possession of it. Our faith must know that it is heard and receives what it asks, and therefore quietly perseveres in its supplication until the answer comes. The true intercessor must be a person of faith.

Prayer And Work

The intercessor must be *a messenger*. He must be prepared to offer himself personally to receive the answer and to dispense it. Praying and working go together. Think of Moses—his boldness in pleading with God for the people was no greater than his pleading with the people for God. We see the same in Elijah—the urgency of his prayer in secret is equaled by his jealousy for God in public, as he witnessed against the sin of the nation. Let intercession always be accompanied by humbly waiting on God to receive His grace and to know more definitely what and how He would have us to work. It is a great thing to begin the work of intercession—the drawing down to earth of the blessings which heaven provides for every need. It is a greater thing as intercessor personally to receive that blessing and go out from God's face knowing that we have secured something that we can impart to someone else. May God make us all

wholehearted, believing intercessors who are prepared to bless others.

Chapter 35

THE TRUE INTERCESSOR

"The effectual fervent prayer of a righteous man availeth much. Elias was a man subject to like passions as we are"—James 5:16,17.

We sometimes see the characters in the Bible as exceptional cases and think that what we see in them is not to be expected of us. The aim of God in Scripture is the very opposite. He gives us these men for our instruction and encouragement, as a specimen of what His grace can do. They are living examples of what His will and our nature at once demand and make possible.

To give confidence to all of us who aim at a life of effectual prayer James wrote: "Elias was a man subject to like passions as we are." There was no difference between his nature and ours, or between the grace that works in him and works in us. There is no reason why we should not, like him, pray effectually. If our prayer is to have power, we must seek to have Elijah's spirit. The desire to pray like Elijah is perfectly legitimate and very necessary. If we honestly seek for the secret of his power in prayer, we must study his life. We shall find it in his life with God, his work for God, his trust in God.

Elijah's Prayers

Prayer is the voice of our life. As a man lives so he prays. It is not the words or thoughts with which he is occupied at set times of prayer, but the condition of his heart as seen in his desires and actions that is regarded by God as his real prayer. The life speaks louder and truer than the lips. To pray well I must live well. He who seeks to live with God will learn to know His mind and to please Him, so that he will be able to pray according to His will.

Elijah, in his first message to Ahab, spoke of "the Lord God, before whom I stand" (1 Kings 17:1). Think of his solitude at the brook Cherith, receiving his bread from God through the ravens, and then at Sarepta through the ministry of a poor widow. He walked with God; he learned to know God well. When the time came, he knew how to pray to a God whom he had proved to be faithful. It is only out of a life of true fellowship with God that the prayer of faith can be born. Let the link between the life and the prayer be clear and close. As we give ourselves to walk with God, we will learn to pray.

Elijah went where God sent him. He did what God commanded him. He stood up for God and His service. He witnessed against the people and their sin. All who heard him could say: "Now I know that thou art a man of God, and that the word of the Lord in thy mouth is truth'' (1 Kings 17:24). His prayers were all in connection with his work for God. He was equally a man of action and a man of prayer. He prayed and the drought came and then the rain. This was part of his prophetic work, so that the people, by judgment and mercy, might be brought back to God. When Elijah prayed down fire from heaven on the sacrifice, it was so that God might be known as the true God. All of his prayers were for the glory of God.

Believers often seek power in prayer so they will be able to get good gifts for themselves. This secret selfishness robs them of the power and the answer. It is when self is lost in the desire for God's glory and our life is devoted to work for God, that power to pray can come. God lives to love, save, and bless men. The believer who gives himself up to God's service will find new life in prayer. Work for others proves the honesty of our prayer for them. Work for God reveals our need and our right to pray boldly. Say to God that you are completely given up to His service. This will strengthen your confidence in His hearing you.

Elijah Trusted God

Elijah had learned to trust God for his personal needs during the famine and he dared trust Him for greater things in answer to prayer for His people. Elijah had confidence that God would hear him when he made his appeal to the God who answers by fire. He had confidence that God would

152

do what he would ask. He announced to Ahab that rain was coming and then, with his face to the earth, pleaded for it, while his servant, six times over, brought the message, "There is nothing" (1 Kings 18:43). Elijah's unwavering confidence in the promise and character of God, and God's personal friendship, gave him power for the effectual prayer of the righteous man.

The inner chamber is the place where this has to be learned. The morning watch is the training school where we are to exercise the grace that can equip us to pray like Elijah. The God of Elijah still lives. The spirit that was in him dwells in us. Let us cease our limited and selfish views of prayer, which only aim at grace enough to keep us standing. Let us cultivate the same awareness that Elijah had of living completely for God, and we will learn to pray like he did. Prayer will bring to us and to others the blessed experience that our prayers are effectual and of great value.

In the power of our Savior, who ever lives to intercede, let us have courage and not fear. We have given ourselves to God; we are working for Him. We are learning to know and trust Him. We can count on the life of God and the Holy Spirit dwelling in us to make us a righteous man whose effectual prayer avails much.